LILLIAN TOO'S
EIGHT CHARACTERS
CHINESE PERSONAL FORECASTING

Discover the secrets of Chinese Destiny Prediction in this complete book by Lillian Too. Simplified as only she can without losing the fascinating essence of this skill, now you can learn how to analyze Paht Chee charts without getting confused by perplexing terminology.

FULLY ILLUSTRATED

KONSEP BOOKS
KONSEP LAGENDA SDN BHD (223 855)
Kuala Lumpur 59100 MALAYSIA

WEBSITES:
www.lillian-too.com
www.wofs.com
www.fsmegamall.com
Email: ltoo@wofs.com

LILLIAN TOO'S
EIGHT CHARACTERS
CHINESE PERSONAL FORECASTING
© Konsep Lagenda Sdn Bhd

ISBN 983-3263-48-8
This edition first published in Malaysia in
September 2005

Revised edition May 2006

This book is dedicated to

Jennifer

and her great team at
World of Feng Shui.

CONTENT

My dear readers,

*T*his book takes a comprehensive look at the EIGHT CHARACTERS chart, which the Chinese use to make personal life forecasting. In Chinese it is known by its literal translation Paht chee and this is popularly referred to as the birth chart that reveals a great deal about one's destiny. The Chinese give life forecasting methods the same respect they give to feng shui. This is because belief in luck is an integral part of the Chinese psyche. So life forecasting is rarely ignored and advice from astrologers and paht chee experts are almost always taken into account when important family decisions are made as

- When a baby is born, an expert is consulted before a name is given.
- When a potential marriage partner appears on the scene for any of their offspring, the astrologer is again consulted to determine the suitability and compatibility of the proposed match.
- When choosing dates for all major celebrations and occasions such as moving house, starting a new venture, getting married, traveling, and so forth.

The Chinese depend most strongly on the vitality of personal paht chee charts which are read in conjunction with the vitality of years, months and days. The underlying belief in Chinese destiny forecasting skills, is the philosophy that prevention is infinitely better than cure. So the Chinese approach is always to try to prevent bad things from happening. Indeed the ultimate reason for consulting experts in these esoteric skills is to enable them to avoid misfortunes.

PERSONAL LIFE FORECASTING

Personal life forecasting starts with learning how to analyze the Eight Characters in your paht chee chart. Each person's chart is different. Using only the five elements of wood, fire, earth, metal and water – with a yin or a yang countenance - the chart can be systematically studied, analyzed, broken down and interpreted to reveal the probabilities of wealth luck, relationships luck, success luck and so forth that our life holds in store for us. When charts are correctly drawn up and interpreted, they are incredibly accurate in forecasting when each of the different kinds of good fortune or misfortune is likely to occur.

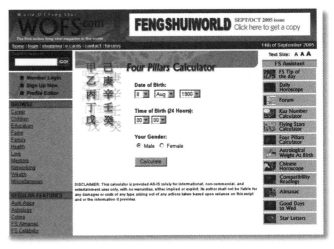

This book concentrates its contents mainly on reading and interpreting the basic paht chee chart itself as well as the ten-year luck period charts. These charts are drawn up according to a formula of computation based on the Chinese lunar calendar. This book does not teach you how to compute these charts. Instead as a free service to all readers, you can access your personal paht chee charts and ten year luck pillars by visiting **www.wofs.com**. Just sign in and download your paht chee charts which we have installed on the wofs website. You can then use this book to read and understand your chart.

The charts computed via the website are derived from the Chinese thousand year calendar, which comprise the heavenly stems, earthly branches, elements and lo shu numbers of each year, month and day of the whole period of a thousand years. It is easier to store all this information in a computer program then to include them in this book. Based on a simple programming method the charts of individuals are calculated within seconds.

SIMPLIFYING THE TERMINOLOGY

Anyone can learn to read the charts and become adept at forecasting their luck and fortunes. It is not difficult once you master the basic fundamentals and you will find this book really easy to understand mainly because, as with my feng shui books, I have simplified the terminology used. You will discover this book is a rather fun way to find out what the future has is in store for you. How adept you eventually become in making accurate predictions depend on how much you practice. As with most skills, practice makes perfect so the more readings you do the faster you will develop a facility with the stems, branches, stars and elements in the charts.

BENEFITS OF KNOWING PAHT CHEE

When you know paht chee you will find yourself becoming exceedingly popular because everyone wants to know their future! It can also be used to analyze the compatibility of people considering marriage, or going into business together or considering employment.

Becoming adept at this skill also enhances your practice of feng shui, because the two are very much complementary living skills. When used correctly they definitely maximize your success potential and happiness.

Having the ability to forecast good and bad years gives anyone a competitive edge in life. Knowing in advance about bad luck periods can be the difference between losing a few dollars or losing several thousand dollars, OR between sustaining a small fall versus getting involved in a big accident. We might not be able to escape experiencing some misfortune in a bad period, but we can, by being careful, and by using element remedies substantially diminish its effect. It is up to you how detailed you wish to be when you delve into what life has in store for you according to your birth data. What you do to enhance the opportunity that shows itself during your benchmark years is in your hands.

How much of your own instincts you add to the process is also up to you. I believe that deep within every human individual are powerful psychic abilities that lie embedded until they get awakened with use. Once surfaced, our higher instincts become increasingly stronger. This is what I have discovered, that the more I analyze eight character charts the sharper my instincts seem to have become over the years.

Destiny however is only one part of the equation of life; there is also the input of one's actions and the influence of one's attitudes. When we are passionate enough about wanting to transform our lives, we usually can also transform our destiny.

In any case fate is only one fifth of our future. Success, health, wealth or happiness are abstractions. How much or how little we have of each depend on ourselves. In the same way, how much we deem is enough is also our own decision. In the end it is what we make of what is given to us that decides the direction and quality of our life.

The ability to make luck forecasts and destiny predictions is to help us improve ourselves; to enhance our lives and make good decisions, and then to extend this help outwards towards the people we love and care about, and even to those we don't care for. These are living skills that aid us, and which enable us to help others. Just like learning to drive, to read, to add, to count, to help people ... they make life and living a whole lot more pleasant and meaningful so they are certainly worth learning.

The challenge to me is to make the learning process interesting without losing the spirit of the knowledge we are dealing with. I have so enjoyed writing, editing and re editing this book and to those of you new to Chinese personal forecasting, I honestly hope I have succeeded in sparking a real interest in you towards this wonderful skill. I also hope it gives you hours of reading pleasure and that ultimately it helps many of you move extra gracefully and happily through life.

Lillian Too
October 2005
Kuala Lumpur, Malaysia

Part One

EIGHT CHARACTERS

IN CHINESE FORTUNE TELLING

INTRODUCTION

The eight characters method in Chinese fortune telling is generally accepted as the most accurate and comprehensive way of looking at one's future destiny. It is a method that uses four important pieces of birth data. These make up the *Four Pillars of destiny* - the Hour, the Day, the Month and the Year of a person's birth - to calculate the person's eight characters or paht chee chart.

The *eight characters* in the chart are the *eight elements* that contain the codes of a person's destiny, a map that shows all the influences of the five elements on the person's life.

It is made up of *four heavenly* stem elements and *four earthly* branch elements that map out a person's destiny. These eight elements are collectively referred to as the basket of elements that offer clues to a person's character, a person's circumstances and his/her potential to enjoy different kinds of good fortune as well as indications of the crosses a person has to bear at different periods of his/her life.

The basket of elements are also analyzed in conjunction with other charts, one, the *ten year luck periods chart* and two, the elements of any given year. Taken together and in the hands of someone who knows

how to read the charts, much can be revealed and very accurately too. This is when pretty accurate predictions can be made for anyone in any given timeframe.

This is the most significant dimension of the eight characters chart – it reveals when different types of good luck will manifest for the person. When expertly interpreted, the luck prediction charts reveal very accurate predictions about the quality and success potential in a person's life, i.e. when the person will rise to success; when important opportunities will open up, when the person will meet someone important and significant, when that person will get married.

In addition the charts also point to dangerous years when the person will need to be careful about health, about being swindled, being too trusting, meeting with an accident and so forth.

To obtain a full picture, the *eight characters* chart must be read in conjunction with the ten-year period pillars as well as take into account the elements and other attributes of the year. These have the most direct influence on one's fortunes based on their interactions with the elements of one's *eight characters* and one's luck pillars.

IMPORTANCE OF FIVE ELEMENTS

*T*he key to unlocking the meanings of paht chee charts is knowledge of the five elements - wood, fire, earth, metal and water - and their cycles of production, destruction and exhaustion. The elements that appear in the chart are further differentiated according to whether they are heavenly stems or earthly branches.

Gaining familiarity with the elements that make up the stems and branches is important because the thousand-year calendar, from which the whole system derives its charts, is expressed in terms of these stems and branches. There are specific Chinese names for each of these stems and branches.

YIN/YANG FORCES
The elements of the stems and branches can be either yin or yang. These are opposing forces, which complement and give life to each other. Yin and yang make up the tai chi principle which stress that having all five elements in a chart is what gives it good balance. But it is also important to see if they are made up of all yin, all yang or a combination of yin and yang pillars.

When there is a shortage or an excess of any element, one's life is supposedly out of balance. Charts with shortages and excesses indicate lives that have its fair share of obstacles and misfortunes UNLESS the shortage or excess is identified, and then properly remedied.

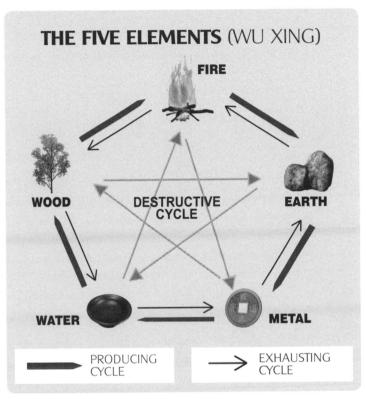

THE FIVE ELEMENTS (WU XING)

FIRE

WOOD

DESTRUCTIVE CYCLE

EARTH

WATER

METAL

➤ PRODUCING CYCLE

→ EXHAUSTING CYCLE

IT IS RARE TO FIND A CHART WITH A PERFECT BALANCE OF ALL FIVE ELEMENTS
This is the first and most simplistic indication of a good life chart. Usually however in most people's paht chee charts there are always some element missing and therefore there will be an excess of some other element. So everyone is likely to suffer from some kind of shortage or excess of a particular element. This is usually interpreted that some kind of affliction, aggravation, disappointment, failure or loss at some point in the person's life is likely to happen. *No one's life is perfect.*

In the old days, as soon as a child is born to a wealthy or prominent family, more so when the child is a son, his eight characters chart is immediately drawn up so the name selected directly addresses the shortage or excess of elements. The remedy is to incorporate the missing element(s) into the name.

Chinese names usually incorporate water, metal, fire, wood or gold.

This way, the child's life instantly becomes better balanced, thereby bringing him good fortune. The naming of children in the old days was thus determined with the help of a trusted family astrologer. The practice continues to this day, amongst traditional Chinese families in Hong Kong, Taiwan and China.

When a person's chart has all five elements present, this is a good indication that the person's life is relatively comfortable, well balanced with more than enough to eat and with reasonable good fortune. It is also this good balance of element forces that will enable the person to benefit from any good fortune specifically indicated in the chart.

USEFULNESS OF PAHT CHEE READING

Getting a paht chee reading gives us advance notice of good and bad times at different ages of a person's life, when misfortunes might occur so advising caution, and when the good years will occur thereby encouraging one to be courageous in taking business, career or relationship risks. The path chee reading of good and bad ten-year periods is especially useful for those running businesses or planning career moves. Changing direction is always auspicious when done at the start of a good ten-year life period. It is definitely bad when one is at the tail end of one's good ten-year period.

To obtain your paht chee and ten-year luck period charts go to **www.wofs.com** and click on the Four pillars chart icon. Register as a member of the site and when the paht chee decoder page comes up, you can fill in your birth details as requested. Your paht chee and luck period charts will appear and you can then print them out for analysis. There is no charge for this service. It is free. By having your charts calculated this way, it will let you focus your full attention on learning how to read your charts.

Armed with the correct chart and this book, anyone can work through their life charts and make specific prophecies about their own life. More important is that even the most amateur practitioner can find out immediately what is 'good" and what is "bad" for them.

My approach to reading the eight characters chart is very simple and straightforward. No one needs to get confused by difficult terminology. This is because instead of using Chinese words to describe the different heavenly stem and earthly branch, my paht chee chart shows the five elements with a yin or a yang essence. In addition the earthly branches are not named in Chinese – instead I use the 12 animals of the Chinese Zodiac and this instantly makes everything easier to remember and understand.

I do this because I believe in simplifying eight characters paht chee; I do not believe I need to make the subject look difficult and confusing. What is important is that the method must be accessible to anyone and everyone.

My advice however is for readers to go through this book once through first, prior to attempting to read their own chart. This will ensure the reader gets a whole picture understanding, otherwise they get distracted by attempting to learn and to read their own chart simultaneously. That will be counter productive to the learning process and could end being very frustrating for the reader.

When you start reading your own chart before you have fully understood the method of analysis you are certain to have too many questions and then, your own frustration will cause you to get distracted or worse, cause you give up before you even start. So go slowly and become familiar with the charts first before you start trying to interpret all the eight characters in the chart.

Walk through the examples in this book with me as you read. This will give you the practice needed in knowing what to look for, in knowing how to determine your self element, knowing how to decide if your self element is weak or strong and knowing how to use this preliminary information to proceed to the next stage of the reading.

Eventually how adept and good you become in making luck predictions about yourself and, about others depends on how familiar you are with the charts and most important of all, how well you understand the theory of the five elements. As with most skills, practice makes perfect. Over time you will become so familiar with the theory of five elements (referred to as wuxing) that interpreting a paht chee chart becomes very easy. If you go slowly you will have no difficulty in attaining the familiarity required.

Paht chee analysis should be used to determine the compatibility of two people considering marriage, or any group of people thinking of going into business together. It is an excellent skill for human resource managers as the chart immediately shows whether potential employees will 'fit' into the culture of the company and whether they will benefit the company, and/or the boss. It is always good to employ people who have just entered into a favourable ten-year luck period, as their good fortune is certain to spill over.

Being able to make life and luck predictions gives anyone a competitive edge. Although good fortune or misfortune is part of everyone's life, nevertheless the measure of good fortune or misfortune is often more important and also more interesting. Happily this aspect of life's developments – the magnitude of good fortune or misfortune - is within one's control.

Knowing when to take precautions and be more careful and when to move bravely forward in taking business or other risks for instance has an important bearing on the extent or severity of our fortunes and misfortunes.

Becoming proficient at making luck predictions will enhance your practice of feng shui, and although fortune telling and feng shui are separate practices requiring different skills, nevertheless they are complementary, and can be used together to good effect.

More importantly these skills alert us to life's afflictions prompting us to deal with them before they occur. For many people this certainly makes for a less aggravating existence. Peace is such a rare commodity these days that anything that can bring more peace into our lives must surely be very welcome.

GENERATING THE CHARTS

*Y*ou can tell a great deal about yourself and about what the future holds for you by looking at the charts. First let us look at the charts and look at how they are generated. You need four pieces of information about your birth.

These are:
YOUR **YEAR** OF BIRTH
Refers to your year of birth according to the lunar Chinese calendar

YOUR **MONTH** OF BIRTH
This reveals the seasonal element of your birth day

YOUR **DAY** OF BIRTH
Refers to your day of birth according to the Chinese calendar

YOUR **HOUR** OF BIRTH
Refers to the hour of birth at your local place of birth.

To create the charts the data needs to be converted into your eight characters which is basically the paht chee chart. It is not necessary to convert your time of birth to Greenwich mean time. It is the time of birth in your locality and country that counts. Thus if you were born at night then your hour of birth must reflect this in the chart. Literally, paht chee means eight words or eight characters.

THE PAHT CHEE CHART

We start by becoming familiar with the Paht chee chart. These two words paht chee means literally eight characters. There are eight characters, two for each PILLAR of the chart. Since there are 4 pillars – year, month, day and hour – there are in total 8 characters.

These eight characters are the names of the ten heavenly stems and the twelve earthly branches which are used to describe the hours, days, months and years of the Chinese lunar calendar. So to construct one's paht chee chart requires one to know the hour, day, month and year of one's birth accurately. It is unnecessary to adjust for international time differences of the different places of birth because one's life is affected by the conditions that prevail during one's birth.

Getting to know the Eight Characters Chart in greater depth

First see how the chart is made up of four vertical columns, which are labeled as a person's FOUR PILLARS. These columns are named HOUR, DAY, MONTH and YEAR. Under each of the vertical headings are two characters, an upper character, which is one of the ten heavenly stems, and a lower character, which is one of the twelve earthly branches – i.e. one of the Chinese animal horoscopes.

Altogether, there are eight characters in a paht chee chart. So the paht chee chart reveals a person's eight elements, four of which are the heavenly stems and four are earthly branches.

The eight characters comprise four pairs of elements (4 X 2 = 8). Each character is described as a pillar made up of two elements, an upper element known as the heavenly stem, and a lower element known as the earthly branch.

The Chinese recognize that the Universe comprise five elements. These are wood, fire, earth, metal and water. These five elements have three cyclical relationships viz:

- A productive cycle
- A destructive cycle and
- An exhaustive cycle

You must be very familiar with these cyclical relationships of the five elements to be able to read the eight character charts. For now take note that the eight characters are made up of these five elements occurring as either heavenly stems or earthly branches.

A TYPICAL EIGHT CHARACTERS CHART is made up of FOUR PILLARS. Each pillar has a heavenly stem element and an earth branch element. This is shown on the next page. The Four Pillars are the Year pillar, the Month pillar, the day pillar and the Hour pillar.

Each pillar comprise a set of two elements which are either yin or yang. If the heavenly stem is yin, the earthly branch is also yin. If the stem is yang the branch will also be yang.

Getting to know the PAHT CHEE (8 Characters) Chart

HOUR HEAVENLY STEM	DAY HEAVENLY STEM	MONTH HEAVENLY STEM	YEAR HEAVENLY STEM

辛　Yin Metal

YIN METAL

This HOUR pillar stands for:
- the CHILDREN
- Old age in life cycle

Examine how this element interacts with the SELF element. When it supports the SELF children are a source of joy. When it clashes, offspring give problem.

壬　Yang Water

YANG WATER

This DAY pillar stands for:
- the SELF (ELEMENT)
- Middle age in life cycle

This is the most important pillar of the chart – you must determine if the SELF element is weak or strong and how it interacts with the surrounding elements.

己　Yin Earth

YIN EARTH

This MONTH pillar stands for
- the PARENTS
- your TEENS in the life cycle

Examine how this element combines with the SELF element. It is good when it supports the SELF and bad when it clashes with the SELF.

乙　Yin Wood

YIN WOOD

This YEAR pillar stands for
- the grandparents
- Childhood in the life cycle

This element has the least influence on the SELF but how it combines or clashes with the other elements fives insights into the reading.

HOUR EARTHLY BRANCH	DAY EARTHLY BRANCH	MONTH EARTHLY BRANCH	YEAR EARTHLY BRANCH

巳　Yin Fire

SNAKE FIRE

This HOUR BRANCH signifies your SON or DAUGHTER

The child whose YEAR of birth corresponds to the animal here will be closest to you. Examine the clashes or combinations with the SELF.

申　Yang Metal

MONKEY METAL

This DAY BRANCH signifies the SPOUSE

How this element interacts with the SELF and with the other elements reveal the influence and strength of the different parties in one's life.

丑　Yin Earth

OX EARTH

This MONTH BRANCH signifies the PARENTS

How this element interacts with the SELF reveals the influence of the parents. This element also reveals the kind of luck parents bring to the SELF.

酉　Yin Metal

ROOSTER METAL

This YEAR BRANCH signifies ANCESTORS

The influences of this element is 'distant' but their impact on the chart can represent a great deal of difference to the overall luck of the SELF.

Here is the paht chee chart of someone born in the year of the wood rooster, during the season of autumn.

We will walk through this chart to help you understand how to begin a reading. So first look closely at the paht chee chart and focus on the elements of each of the characters that make up the chart. Note that the heavenly stems are on the top row while the earthly branches – or animal signs are on the bottom row.

When you are sufficiently familiar with the chart we can proceed to analyze the chart.

AT A GLANCE:

The more balanced a chart is the better so ideally it should have all five of the elements present. This is the best indication of a good life. The sample chart shown above has all five elements present so this is a well-balanced chart. However if your chart shows some missing elements it does not mean yours is a bad life. The majority of people have missing elements in their chart. Once you know however you can immediately do something about it. For instance if you are lacking water, having a pond or pool near you will benefit you and putting the word 'water' into your name would benefit you. This could be words that mean the sea, the lake, rain and so forth.

There should ideally be yin as well as yang pillars as this also brings balance to the chart. When the chart is all yin or all yang, the chart is said to be unbalanced. Thus if all four of your pillars are yin ie all the stem and all the branches are yin it suggests a life lacking in yang chi energy. You should make up for this by systematically introducing yang elements into your surroundings such as noise level (like keeping your radio and television turned on,); increasing the amount of light in your surroundings, use yang colours such as white or red around you and create a lifestyle that is highly sociable i.e. where people visit you frequently. All this creates yang chi that will benefit you as it balances out your chart. The chart on the facing page has one yang pillar and three yin pillars and this is fine because both yin and yang are present.

The earthly branches are said to be good and beneficial when all four animal signs belong to the same affinity groups and are not hostile to each other. This is based on the astrological grouping of friends and allies. The chart here shows affinity between the rooster, the snake and the ox which form a triangle of affinity. These three signs indicate this person is a deep thinker or philosopher because these three animals are the thinkers of the Chinese Zodiac. More, the remaining animal sign is the Monkey which is the secret friend of the Snake. So here the earthly branches indicate good relationships in this person's life.

• The heavenly stems are better when they are in a productive relationship rather than a destructive relationship. When the stem elements harmonize it suggests positive relationships and good family harmony. When they are hostile, it suggests underlying tensions. In the sample chart shown here metal produces water, and water produces wood so there is some harmony here.

These are things that can be picked up form the chart at a quick glance and this is useful to do before proceeding to undertake a more in depth analysis.

MISSING ELEMENTS?

Here is another chart which has missing elements. When you look at a chart the first thing to do is count the number of each element and see if there are any elements missing. In the chart on the following page, there are 3 metals, 2 earth, 2 wood, and 1 fire.

In this example chart note there is a missing element, which is water. Instantly we know that this person will benefit by

having water in his/her name; will benefit by living near water, and that the element water will improve his life by balancing the elements. Later when we delve deeper we will be able to see exactly how crucial is the element of water, and what kind of luck, the element of water stands for this person.

YIN OR YANG?

Next note that the elements may be yin or yang, depending on what kind of element character they are. There are altogether a total of ten heavenly stems and these comprise the five elements occurring either as yin or yang. So there is yin wood and yang wood, yin fire and yang fire and so forth. There are altogether, twelve earthly branches and in a more familiar form these are the twelve horoscope animals that we are already so familiar with. Each of these animals also has a designated element, which is again either yin or yang.

The yin and yang aspects of the elements will aid in the analysis later. A chart should ideally have a balance of yin and yang pillars. When all the pillars are yin (as is the case with the example chart here) , this person is sorely in need of yang energy. Which means this person benefits from noise, activity, being in well-lighted areas and benefits from living in warm rather than cold countries. When a chart has all yang characters the person benefits from peace and quiet. Good combinations between yin and yang exert stronger influences while clashes between yin and yang are less strong than between two yins and two yangs.

SELF-ELEMENT

Next, from the chart you have to determine your self-element. The self-element plays a very large part in the reading. The self-element is the element indicated as the heavenly stem of the Day pillar i.e. it is the element in the upper grid of the DAY pillar. In our example the self element is Yin WOOD. The self element unlocks for us what the other elements in the eight character chart stands for and since there are five elements in all, the self element will reveal five aspects of luck for each individual person.

The self-element will reveal the state of a person's wealth luck, your friends/foes luck, your power and vitality luck, your intelligence and creativity luck and your resources luck. We will examine these five types of luck in greater depth as we analyze the charts further in the next chapter,

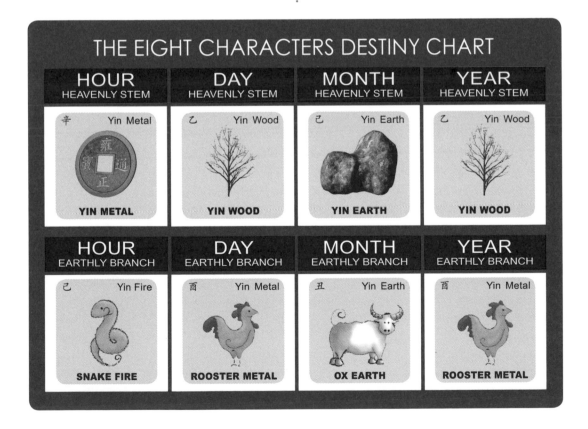

THE EIGHT CHARACTERS DESTINY CHART

HOUR HEAVENLY STEM	DAY HEAVENLY STEM	MONTH HEAVENLY STEM	YEAR HEAVENLY STEM
辛 Yin Metal	乙 Yin Wood	己 Yin Earth	乙 Yin Wood
YIN METAL	**YIN WOOD**	**YIN EARTH**	**YIN WOOD**

HOUR EARTHLY BRANCH	DAY EARTHLY BRANCH	MONTH EARTHLY BRANCH	YEAR EARTHLY BRANCH
己 Yin Fire	酉 Yin Metal	丑 Yin Earth	酉 Yin Metal
SNAKE FIRE	**ROOSTER METAL**	**OX EARTH**	**ROOSTER METAL**

IS SELF ELEMENT WEAK OR STRONG

Next it is necessary to determine if your self-element is weak or strong. When the self element is weak, then it will need the element that produces it to be present before the person can manifest whatever good luck is shown in his chart. For example if the chart shows that the person has wealth luck, this wealth can only manifest if the self-element is made strong.

For example if the self-element is wood and it is weak then it needs water element to strengthen it. If the self element is earth, and it is weak, then it needs fire element to strengthen it. The water element or fire element that is needed can appear in the luck periods chart or it can appear in the year chart e.g. the year 2006 is a fire earth year. So in 2006 anyone needing fire or earth to strengthen its weak self-element will benefit from that year.

When the self element is weak however, then whenever it appears either in the other pillars of the paht chee chart, or in the luck pillars chart or in any year, it signifies that there are friends around to help. Having friends is also interpreted as strengthening the self-element.

When the self-element is strong, the person will find it easier to enjoy the luck indicated by the other elements. But often when the self element is strong, it indicates that there are many false friends around. There is jealousy and hidden envy. If the strong self-element is wood then when wood appears it will always means that the person will have competition. True friends are also hard to come by. They are few and far between.

WHEN IS THE ELEMENT WEAK OR STRONG?

The self element is weak when it is either exhausted or destroyed by many of the other elements around the self element, thereby weakening it. You need to count how many of the remaining 7 elements are weakening the self-element and how many are strengthening it.

The self-element is strong when the surrounding elements strengthen it by either producing it or being the same element as the self element.

Note that the elements of the HOUR and MONTH pillars are closer to the self-element and thus exert greater influence on whether the self-element is weak or strong.

When you are in doubt, look at the elements in the MONTH pillar as these will exert the greatest effect on the strength or weakness of the self element.

The paht chee chart is a destiny chart. It shows the inherent character of a person, the potential he or she is born with, the environment, which he or she grows up in, the influences that will dominate his or her life. All of this is expressed as elements so the entire luck prediction exercise is based on the theory of the five elements.

Everything is revealed according to a person's self element, and how weak or strong it is. Based on this, the chart will indicate if a person has the destiny to become rich, (and if so, it identifies the probable source of wealth); the chart indicates whether one's wealth luck gets better with age or if wealth gets lost. All the manifestations of good fortune and misfortune are reflected in the charts. This requires an interpretation of the elements in both the eight characters and the set of ten-year luck pillars but first let us look more closely at the eight characters chart.

HOW THE PAHT CHEE CHART IS CREATED

The eight characters chart is created from the Chinese calendar. This sets out the heavenly stem and earthly branch characters (or elements) of one's date of birth expressed as the day, the month and the year. So you obtain three sets of elements – one set each for the YEAR, MONTH, and DAY that make up the date of birth from the calendar. This is done by converting your western date of birth to its equivalent date as presented in the Chinese lunar calendar.

As it is cumbersome and rather complicated pouring through the Chinese thousand-year calendar, we have copied all the information in the thousand-year calendar and placed them into a computer software program, which has the formula to convert a western date of birth into a Chinese date. The software program was written to instantly call up the three sets of elements required from your DAY, MONTH and YEAR of birth.

Next we address the HOUR of birth. The earthly branch element of the HOUR is extracted from the table shown on the next page. It is the heavenly stem of the DAY pillar that determines the heavenly stem of your HOUR of birth. This fourth pillar makes up the full four pillars paht chee chart.

Learning how to create the paht chee chart has, in today's world of hi tech wizardry, been reduced to the click of a button. Thus those of you wishing to get your full eight characters chart (and luck pillars), please go to www.wofs.com and register as a bona fide user. You can then get your very own eight characters and luck pillars chart calculated and printed in less than a minute.

The eight characters OR paht chee calculator software on our Internet website has been programmed not to adjust time back to GMT since destiny depends on the time prevailing where you were born. By adjusting the time you could well be turning night into day and vice versa. So the chart generated

THE TWELVE EARTHLY BRANCHES OF HOURS

HOURS	NAME OF HOURS	
11pm - 1am	子	Rat - Yang Water
1am - 3am	丑	Ox - Yin Earth
3am - 5am	寅	Tiger - Yang Wood
5am - 7am	卯	Rabbit - Yin Wood
7am - 9am	辰	Dragon - Yang Earth
9am - 11am	巳	Snake - Yin Fire
11am - 1pm	午	Horse - Yang Fire
1pm - 3pm	未	Sheep - Yin Earth
3pm - 5pm	申	Monkey - Yang Metal
5pm - 7pm	酉	Rooster - Yin Metal
7pm - 9pm	戌	Dog - Yang Earth
9pm - 11pm	亥	Boar - Yin Water

THE HOUR PILLAR IN THE CHART

The HOUR pillar in Paht chee comprise a heavenly stem and an earthly branch. The stem of the HOUR has to be worked out based on a formula. The earthly branch of one's hour of birth is based on the actual time of birth recorded. In an 24 hour day comprising night and day hours, every two hour period is represented by an animal sign (or earthly branch.) This is shown in the table above. Note that the HOUR pillar of paht chee charts should use one's time of birth as recorded in one's country of birth. The HOUR of birth should never be adjusted to Greenwich mean time or American standard time. By so doing one can end up turning one's time of birth from night time hours to day time hours and then the reading will be inaccurate. If the chart has the HOUR pillar missing (because you do not know the time of birth), the chart reading is considered incomplete and readings can then be inaccurate.

is based on your hour of birth where you were physically born, not time as measured according to Greenwich mean time.

TEN YEAR LUCK PILLARS

In addition to the paht chee chart there are also the ten-year luck pillars and these are expressed as a pair of elements in every ten-year period of your life. These give very accurate indications of the timing of luck arrival in one's life when one knows how to decipher the interaction of the elements in the luck pillars with that of the eight characters chart.

First note that arising from the SELF element one is already able to determine from the eight characters chart those elements that are favourable and those that are unfavourable to one's destiny luck. When the favourable elements in the yin or yang aspect show up in the ten-year luck pillars and these also correspond to favourable elements of a calendar year, then that will be the year when a rise in fortunes will occur.

The chart offers clues on when any rise to prominence or to wealth is most likely to happen. So if you wish to look for signs of good fortune ripening in your life you must first determine the elements that are "favourable" for you.

The ten-year luck pillars is always read in conjunction with the ruling elements of each calendar year to determine whether the year will bring good, bad or neutral luck. When you know how to interpret the elements correctly, you can predict when a person will attain the high point of his/her life just by looking at the ten-year luck pillars. The ten-year luck pillars warn when will be your low period and that will be when you should lie low. This is when the elements are unfavourable to you, and that is when danger, obstacles and misfortunes can aggravate your life.

The website www.wofs.com will also generate your ten-year luck pillars. On the next page is an example of the luck pillars. You will see that this comprises the two elements that rule your destiny during consecutive ten-year periods.

The starting years of the ten-year luck pillars and elements generated for each pillar are derived from a special formula using your gender and your date of birth. From the years indicated you should calculate out how old you are at each of the ten years represented by each of the luck pillars.

Overleaf is what a typical ten year luck pillars chart looks like. Note how each luck pillar represents a ten-year period, and how each pillar is made up of two elements. The two elements comprise the heavenly stem and earthly branch elements in consecutive ten year periods of your life The upper part of the chart shows the heavenly stem character and this is said to be the first five years of that ten year period while the lower portion shows the earthly branch or

10 YEAR LUCK PERIODS OF THE DESTINY CHART

1946 - 1952	1953 - 1962	1963 - 1972	1973 - 1982	1983 - 1992	1993 - 2002
1-7 years	8-17 years	18-27 years	28-37 years	38-47 years	48-57 years
己 Yin Earth	庚 Yang Metal	辛 Yin Metal	壬 Yang Water	癸 Yin Water	甲 Yang Wood
丑 Yin Earth	寅 Yang Wood	卯 Yin Wood	辰 Yang Earth	巳 Yin Fire	午 Yang Fire

lower portion shows the earthly branch or horoscope animal which signifies the next five years of the ten year period.

If you wish to generate your personal paht chee chart and ten year luck pillars, go to **www.wofs.com** at your computer, then fill in your birth details as well as your hour of birth. You will then generate a set of charts which you can start to analyze. Look at your own charts and take note of the elements of the heavenly stems and earthly branches of the paht chee. Note if the elements are yin or yang. Next look at your luck pillars paying attention to the elements indicated.

While the paht chee indicates the strength, weaknesses and the potential that every person is born with, the luck potential pillars indicate the energy influences that will prevail in each ten year period that will cause the good influences or bad influences of the paht chee to manifest good or bad luck. So the two charts must be read together.

Like the eight characters chart, the luck pillars are also expressed as elements, which can strengthen or weaken the person's paht chee elements. When the elements of the luck pillars trigger off the paht chee's wealth potential, that is when the person will enter into a 'rich period" ie the ten years of his/her life when he/she is likely to get rich.

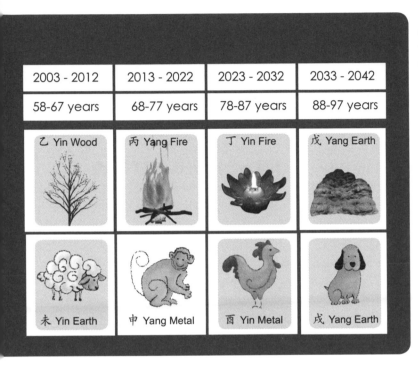

2003 - 2012	2013 - 2022	2023 - 2032	2033 - 2042
58-67 years	68-77 years	78-87 years	88-97 years
乙 Yin Wood	丙 Yang Fire	丁 Yin Fire	戊 Yang Earth
未 Yin Earth	申 Yang Metal	酉 Yin Metal	戌 Yang Earth

This is an example of the Ten Year Luck Pillars which reveal the elements that dominate every ten year period of one's life destiny.

When read in conjunction with the Paht Chee Chart and the calendar years, it provides a comprehensive picture of one's luck during each of the ten years luck periods.

When we say a person has a "good" set of luck pillars, we mean that the pillars during the ages of around 30 to 50 years have elements that provide the missing element (s) of the eight characters chart i.e. elements that fill in what is lacking in the chart OR it stands for wealth luck coming. So you must first determine which are the elements that are deemed good for you before you can read the luck pillars chart correctly. You also need to identify the elements of the chart, which represent wealth and other kinds of luck. More on this later.

A GOOD CHART

So for a chart to indicate success, wealth, happiness or health, we need not only a well balanced and lucky set of elements in the eight characters chart, we also need a set of luck pillars that support and strengthen, or balance, the elements of the eight characters chart. The ten-year luck pillars simply must indicate favourable elements that can support the person's weak SELF-element for it to be considered good.

The elements of the luck pillars exert such a strong influence that they can cause a lucky eight characters chart to lack the strength to bring auspicious success to the person. Or it can also bring fantastic success to a person with an apparently weak eight characters chart to enjoy immense success. So the luck pillars offer crucial inputs into a person's success and happiness potential.

Often, when the elements in the luck pillars are favourable they will more than compensate for any weakness in the eight characters chart. They are then said to remedy imbalances in the eight characters chart.

The key to a successful reading therefore is to examine the ten-year luck pillars closely and see at what age the favourable elements required to strengthen or balance the eight characters chart make an appearance. If the required favourable elements do not make an appearance at all, then success and happiness can be elusive.

CALENDAR YEARS

However all is not lost because then we will look at the elements of calendar years for these too exert their influence on our destiny. When the elements of the calendar years are favourable the year brings good fortune. It stands to reason therefore that when both the luck pillars and the calendar years show favourable elements, then that is when we will enjoy fantastic luck! Those years do not come often and definitely do not come for everyone. This is the difference between having a good chart or being born with an unfavourable chart.

So do take note that the elements of calendar years can strengthen or balance the elements in the eight characters chart. Generally however if the elements in the luck pillars are unfavourable they are usually strong enough to cause misfortune to occur; or to prevent good luck from manifesting. Here is where those who know about the shortcomings in their luck pillars can do something about it. This means you can surround yourself with objects, colours and so forth that signify the favourable element needed to improve your luck.

TEN HEAVENLY STEMS

The Chinese names of the stems and branches are the "characters" of the paht chee chart. Shown here are the Chinese names of the ten heavenly stem characters, their corresponding element and their yin or yang aspect. The stems actually comprise the

THE TEN HEAVENLY STEMS

	HEAVENLY STEMS		
HS 1	Jia	甲	Yang Wood
HS 2	Yi	乙	Yin Wood
HS 3	Bing	丙	Yang Fire
HS 4	Ding	丁	Yin Fire
HS 5	Wu	戊	Yang Earth
HS 6	Ji	己	Yin Earth
HS 7	Geng	庚	Yang Metal
HS 8	Xin	辛	Yin Metal
HS 9	Ren	壬	Yang Water
HS 10	Gui	癸	Yin Water

RELATIVES IN THE PAHT CHEE

HOUR PILLAR	DAY PILLAR	MONTH PILLAR	YEAR PILLAR
Heavenly Stem	Heavenly Stem	Heavenly Stem	Heavenly Stem
Earthly Branch	Earthly Branch	Earthly Branch	Earthly Branch
Children	Self & Spouse	Parents	Grandparents
Old Age	Middle Age	Youth	Childhood

five elements manifesting in either a yin or a yang aspect. These names are generic to the Chinese calendar and have no other meaning. In Chinese books on eight characters, and in the calendar, elements are always referred to by these names.

The elements are placed here in the conventional order of the producing cycle, starting with wood.

Wood produces fire, which produces earth, which produces metal, which in turn produces water. And then water produces wood and the cycle starts again.

Learning the names of these characters is quite useful although it is the recognition of the element with its yin or yang aspect that is more important. Knowing the names of the ten stems makes it possible for you to understand the lunar calendar but it does not necessarily make analyzing the charts any easier.

What does make analysis easier is to understand that the heavenly stems are simply the five elements with either a Yin nature or a YANG nature. Note that all the odd numbered stems are yang and all the even numbered stems are yin.

Later when we analyze the eight characters chart, we have to look out for how the elements of the heavenly stems in each of the four pillars - Hour, Day, Month and Year in the chart either combine or clash with each other. When the elements combine it suggests the outcome is good, when the elements clash it suggests the outcome is bad. When the combination or clash is between two yang or two yin stems, the result is magnified and in the case of clashes it is more severe.

For now take note that each of the pillars Hour, Day, Month, Year stands for different members of the family and for different periods of one's life. This is illustrated in the table on this page.

The eight characters chart is read by looking at how the stem element of each pillar interact with its neighbour. When it is combining harmoniously as in a productive relationship the reading is positive. When the elements clash the reading is negative. In the section on chart interpretation therefore we will investigate what the clashes and combinations of stem elements mean and how they relate to one's luck.

EARTHLY BRANCHES

Next we look at the earthly branches, which make up the four characters in the bottom half of the paht chee chart. There are 12 branches and these are the twelve animal signs of the Chinese Zodiac. The earthly branches have Chinese names as well as equivalent horoscope animal and corresponding element (also with a yin or a yang aspect). The heavenly stems and earthly branches make up the Chinese calendar. It will be easier if you think of the earthly branches as the 12 animals of the Chinese astrological zodiac. Each of the animals have an intrinsic element. There are two animals having each of the elements metal, water, wood and fire with either a yin or a yang nature; and there are four animal signs, which have earth as their element. Two of these are yin and two are yang. The 12 animal signs or earthly branches are illustrated in the chart here. Their Chinese names are also given here for your information.

As with the heavenly stems, when we read the eight characters it is necessary to look at how the elements of the earthly branches combine. When they combine in a positive way the outcome is good and when they clash the outcome is negative. We will study the combinations and clashes in detail in the next chapter. There are also hidden stems in the branches and these will add extra dimensions to the reading.

THE EARTHLY BRANCHES

EARTHLY BRANCHES			
EB 1	Zi	子	Rat - Yang Water
EB 2	Chou	丑	Ox - Yin Earth
EB 3	Yin	寅	Tiger - Yang Wood
EB 4	Mao	卯	Rabbit - Yin Wood
EB 5	Chen	辰	Dragon - Yang Earth
EB 6	Si	巳	Snake - Yin Fire
EB 7	Wu	午	Horse - Yang Fire
EB 8	Wei	未	Sheep - Yin Earth
EB 9	Shen	申	Monkey - Yang Metal
EB 10	You	酉	Rooster - Yin Metal
EB 11	Xu	戌	Dog - Yang Earth
EB 12	Hai	亥	Boar - Yin Water

Part Two

ANALYZING
THE
PAHT CHEE
OR
EIGHT
CHARACTERS
CHART

THE SELF ELEMENT

WHY IT IS SO IMPORTANT IN YOUR READING

Begin your paht chee analysis by determining your SELF ELEMENT. This is an important first step to unlocking the influences that shape your life destiny because everything you want to know about:

- whether you will become wealthy,
- about what kind of success you can attain,
- your likely partner(s) and the kind of marriage you will have,
- when you will meet your life partner,
- the state of your health,
- your family and everything else related to success at what you do – are derived from your self element, whether it is weak or strong, and how it interacts with the other elements in the chart to reveal the secrets of your destiny. So we start by identifying our self element.

SAMPLE CHART READING

In the eight characters chart, this is the heavenly stem of the DAY pillar. So in the example chart illustrated here, the SELF-element is YIN WOOD. Having identified your SELF ELEMENT, the next thing is to determine if it is weak or strong.

The strength of the SELF ELEMENT determines the elements that will be favourable for you as well as the elements, which will hinder or block your success. In paht chee reading, no single element is "good" or "bad".

Everything depends on how the elements of the chart interact with the self-element and with each other, and more particularly, how they interact with the elements that make up your ten year luck pillars. More it also depends on how they interact with the elements of each calendar year.

It is the result of these interactions (or combinations) that enable accurate predictions of good fortune and misfortunes to be predicted during particular years. Implicit in this therefore is that you must develop an easy familiarity with the five elements and their relationship with each other if you want to unlock the meanings of the eight characters and the luck pillars.

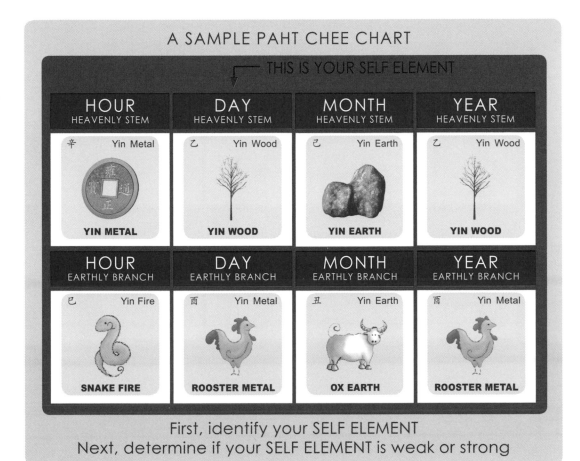

A SAMPLE PAHT CHEE CHART

THIS IS YOUR SELF ELEMENT

HOUR HEAVENLY STEM	DAY HEAVENLY STEM	MONTH HEAVENLY STEM	YEAR HEAVENLY STEM
Yin Metal **YIN METAL**	Yin Wood **YIN WOOD**	Yin Earth **YIN EARTH**	Yin Wood **YIN WOOD**

HOUR EARTHLY BRANCH	DAY EARTHLY BRANCH	MONTH EARTHLY BRANCH	YEAR EARTHLY BRANCH
Yin Fire **SNAKE FIRE**	Yin Metal **ROOSTER METAL**	Yin Earth **OX EARTH**	Yin Metal **ROOSTER METAL**

First, identify your SELF ELEMENT
Next, determine if your SELF ELEMENT is weak or strong

You must determine whether the SELF-element is weak or strong correctly because this has significant ramifications on the subsequent readings. Examine the other elements that surround the self-element and see how they affect the WOOD of the self-element.

1. First look at the HS of the MONTH pillar. Here it is YIN EARTH . Since Wood controls Earth it does not hurt WOOD.
2. Next look at the EB of the DAY pillar. Here it is METAL rooster. The METAL hurts WOOD here.
3. Thirdly look at the HOUR pillar elements. Here the HS is METAL which cuts WOOD and the EB is FIRE which exhausts WOOD.

We can conclude from the above that the SELF ELEMENT of WOOD is definitely WEAK

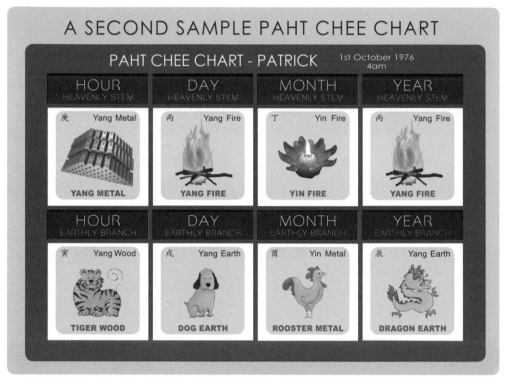

A SECOND SAMPLE PAHT CHEE CHART

PAHT CHEE CHART - PATRICK
1st October 1976
4am

HOUR HEAVENLY STEM	DAY HEAVENLY STEM	MONTH HEAVENLY STEM	YEAR HEAVENLY STEM
庚 Yang Metal **YANG METAL**	丙 Yang Fire **YANG FIRE**	丁 Yin Fire **YIN FIRE**	丙 Yang Fire **YANG FIRE**

HOUR EARTHLY BRANCH	DAY EARTHLY BRANCH	MONTH EARTHLY BRANCH	YEAR EARTHLY BRANCH
寅 Yang Wood **TIGER WOOD**	戌 Yang Earth **DOG EARTH**	酉 Yin Metal **ROOSTER METAL**	辰 Yang Earth **DRAGON EARTH**

ANOTHER EXAMPLE:

Here is another example of a paht chee chart. This is the chart of Patrick, a young man born in the year of the fire dragon i.e. in 1976. Looking at his chart above we can see that his SELF ELEMENT is YANG FIRE.

To determine if this FIRE is weak or strong we note the following.

1. First we note that the HS of the MONTH pillar is YIN FIRE.
2. Next we note that the EB of the DAY pillar is EARTH which exhausts FIRE.
3. Thirdly we look at the HOUR pillar elements. Here the HS is METAL, which is controlled by FIRE, and the EB is WOOD, which feeds fire.

In this chart the SELF ELEMENT is weakened by METAL and EARTH but is strengthened by WOOD and FIRE. Here it is harder to determine the strength of the SELF-element. In such a situation, we examine the MONTH of birth further. Here it is October, the season of autumn.

From the chart here we see that FIRE in autumn is weak. So Patrick's SELF ELEMENT is weak FIRE. Since determining whether the SELF-element is weak or strong is such an important first step in eight characters reading, you must endeavour to get it absolutely correct. So when you are in doubt, count the elements of the chart that support and strengthen the self-element before making up your mind.

Place weighting on the season of birth based on the Table below which describes the strength of the elements in the seasons. So if your SELF-element is WOOD being born in the Spring makes you STRONG, while being born in the AUTUMN instantly makes you very weak.

Your season of birth is shown in the EARTHLY BRANCH of the MONTH pillar. There are paht chee experts who strongly maintain that the season of birth is the determining factor when deciding whether a SELF-element is weak or strong. This means that once you determine your self-element you next look at the EB element of your Month pillar. If this element supports the self element (either produces it or is the same element) then the self element is strong. If the season element exhausts or destroys the self-element then the self element is weak. According to this school of interpretation, it is only after you have determined the season element and if you are still uncertain that you look at the other surrounding elements.

Another way to determine the effect of the season on the self element is to identify the element of the season itself, whether it is yin or yang. Use the table on the next page to determine the season element. This method also shows how the earth element is accounted for. Usually each season comprise three months and the third month of each of the four seasons is said to be an earth element. Note however that earth is considered a neutral element and its presence and influence will prevail throughout the year.

STRENGTH OF ELEMENTS IN THE SEASONS

	METAL	WOOD	WATER	FIRE
SPRING	VERY WEAK	VERY STRONG	WEAK	STRONG
SUMMER	STRONG	WEAK	VERY WEAK	VERY STRONG
AUTUMN	VERY STRONG	VERY WEAK	STRONG	WEAK
WINTER	WEAK	STRONG	VERY STRONG	VERY WEAK

DETERMINING THE SEASONAL ELEMENT IN DIFFERENT MONTHS

SEASON	FIRST MONTH	SECOND MONTH	THIRD MONTH
SPRING	4th Feb to 6 March **Yang WOOD Tiger**	6th March to 5th April **Yin WOOD Rabbit**	5th April to 6th May **Yang EARTH Dragon**
SUMMER	6th May to 6th June **Yin FIRE Snake**	6th June to 7th July **Yang FIRE Horse**	7th July to 8th August **Yin EARTH Sheep**
AUTUMN	8th Aug to 8th Sept **Yang METAL Monkey**	8th Sep to 8th Oct **Yin METAL Rooster**	8th Oct to 7th Nov **Yang EARTH Dog**
WINTER	7th Nov to 7th Dec **Yin WATER Pig**	7th Dec to 6th Jan **Yang WATER Rat**	6th Jan to 4th Feb **Yin EARTH Ox**

SO TAKE NOTE:

If your self element is wood, and you are born in the first & second months of Spring the wood element is strong and growing. It brings you prosperity luck and it strengthens your self element. This is also the best time of the year to make your important decisions, start your important projects and celebrate your happiness occasions such as getting married, partying for your birthdays and even having children. If you are born in the third month of Spring however, earth's influence is neutral. Wood element people generally thrive in the Spring and winter months and are weak in the summer months. This effect on their luck is more severe if their self element is weak and less so if their self element is strong.

If you are born in the summer any success you earn comes only with hard work. Fire exhausts your energy. If you are born in the autumn you need plenty of help as the season of birth hurts you.

If you are born in the winter, during the first and second months you will be nurtured by water. In your life whenever you go through a difficult time, you can expect to get some kind of reprieve or help during the winter months, unless you already have too much water in your chart in which case instead of helping you, water becomes excessive and could hurt you. When you have wood as your self-element and it is strong wood then water is of not much use as you are likely to have enough of it already.

If your self element is fire and you are born in the first two months of summer the fire element is strong and there is harvesting luck. Summer is the season when flowers bloom and seeds get formed. It is a time for reaping the rewards of your work. This would be a good time for you to celebrate, to get married and to make important decisions.

If you are born in the third month of summer however, the earth element will exhaust you.

The exhausting effect is less strong if your self-element is Yang fire. However if earth is a favourable element for you then the effect of earth will be positive; nevertheless it will still exhaust your energies. If you are born in the spring months, the wood element of the Spring months will nurture you bringing you sustenance. If you are born in autumn or winter, the seasonal effect on your life is more likely to be negative. Those with weak fire as their self element will always need to be careful in the winter months. If they are strong fire people however, winter months will tend to help them by curbing their excess fire.

If your self element is water, and you are born in the first two months of winter then this is the season that will bring you wealth and prosperity. Everywhere there is snow and water and this will strengthen you, more so if you are a weak water person. If you are born in the third month of winter

the effect of earth is neutral but there is the possibility it could hurt you.

The earth of winter is Yin earth so any negative impact it may have on you is severe if your self element is also Yin. If it is yang, the effect is much less. Those whose self-element is water will thrive in the winter months and will have less vitality during the spring and summer. In the spring they will tend to feel drained by their work.

If your self element is metal and you are born in the first two months of Autumn then this season will bring you plenty of success and victory luck. In autumn the metal element reigns supreme – this is the right time of the year to make your important decisions and start your important projects. It is also a good time to get married. Those with metal as their self element will also find these autumn months to be their best time of the year (even if they are not born in autumn). If you are born in the third month however you will come under the influence of the earth element which is good for weak metal people as earth nurtures metal.

If your self element is earth, then the influence of the seasons impact on you all through the year. Whether a season is good or not for you will depend on whether your self element is weak or strong. If it is weak then the summer months will be excellent for you since fire will enhance earth, while the spring months will not be as good.

IMPORTANCE OF SURROUNDING ELEMENTS

*I*t is always necessary to consider the influence of the elements that surround the self element. Since the self element is the DAY stem, then those elements nearest to it exerts the most influence. The elements of the Month and Hour pillars exert more impact on the self element than the elements of the Year pillar.

The strength or weakness of the self element plays a very important role in the overall conclusions of the whole exercise of destiny analysis because it is this that will determine your favourable and unfavourable elements. It determines what years and what months will bring you luck and what years and what months will cause you distress.

If you are unsure of your season and thus of your seasonal element you can use another method to determine your season. Look for any of the following three animal combinations that result in one of the four seasons. These animal signs can be on any of the pillars Hour, Day. Month or Year. If any of the these sets of three animals are present, then they will create the season and corresponding element indicated.

Three seasonal branch combinations:
1. When Tiger, Rabbit & Dragon are present the season is Spring (wood)
2. When Snake, Horse & Sheep are present the season is Summer (fire)

3. When Monkey, Rooster & Dog are present the season is Autumn (Metal)
4. When Pig, Rat & Ox are present the season is Winter (water)

When these combinations are not present you must rely on the Earth Branch element of the month to determine the seasonal element.

A THIRD EXAMPLE

*L*et us look at another example. Here we see the eight characters chart of Jessica, a young lady born in the year of the earth sheep i.e. in 1979. Looking at her chart here we can see that her SELF ELEMENT is YANG WOOD.

To determine if this WOOD is weak or strong we note the following.

1. First we note that the HS of the MONTH pillar is YANG WOOD so it complements the SELF.
2. Next the EB of the DAY/MONTH pillars are EARTH so WOOD controls these. This also tells us that the season of birth is the third month of autumn and Jessica's self element is influenced by yang earth (Dog). The effect is neutral.
3. Thirdly we look at the HOUR pillar elements. Here the HS is EARTH which is subdued by WOOD and the EB is FIRE which exhausts WOOD. So these elements also weaken the self-element of WOOD.

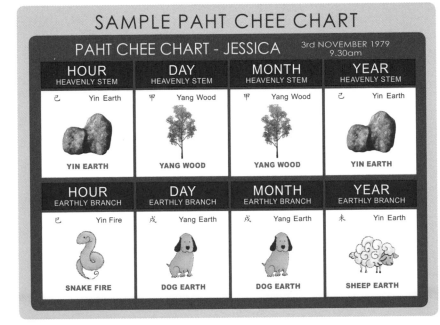

SAMPLE PAHT CHEE CHART

PAHT CHEE CHART - JESSICA   3rd NOVEMBER 1979
9.30am

HOUR HEAVENLY STEM	DAY HEAVENLY STEM	MONTH HEAVENLY STEM	YEAR HEAVENLY STEM
己 Yin Earth	甲 Yang Wood	甲 Yang Wood	己 Yin Earth
YIN EARTH	YANG WOOD	YANG WOOD	YIN EARTH

HOUR EARTHLY BRANCH	DAY EARTHLY BRANCH	MONTH EARTHLY BRANCH	YEAR EARTHLY BRANCH
巳 Yin Fire	戌 Yang Earth	戌 Yang Earth	未 Yin Earth
SNAKE FIRE	DOG EARTH	DOG EARTH	SHEEP EARTH

In this chart, note the missing elements are metal and water. This lady was born in November when WOOD is very weak, in need of both water and metal. Water to nurture and metal to strengthen the water!

So she will benefit from success during her years when metal and water occur in the ten year luck pillars and in the calendar years.

Jessica was born in November, the season of Autumn, which is when WOOD is very weak. So it appears that all the elements point to Jessica's SELF-element being weak WOOD. She is one person who will benefit from WATER, and this is the element that is missing from her chart.

If her ten-year luck period pillars show years with WATER (or Metal because METAL produces water) then Jessica will enjoy big money luck during those years. This is because Jessica's wealth luck element is EARTH and there are five earth elements in her chart. So here is a chart, which has excess EARTH – Jessica cannot become wealthy UNLESS her self is strengthened. If Jessica has plenty of water in her surroundings and has WATER in her ten year luck pillars, she will benefit from the wealth indicators in her paht chee chart. Looking at the chart however the potential of wealth appears elusive. If she builds a swimming pool near where she lives, she will become very rich. I know this because there are wealth indications as evidenced by the presence of earth elements (her wealth element). *Wealth and other kinds of luck indicators are discussed in the next chapter.*

Knowing the SELF ELEMENT enables us to determine important LUCK indicator elements, after which we can check if these elements are present in the chart.

Knowing the strength of the SELF-element enables us to identify the elements that are favourable, and those that are harmful to us.

A FOURTH EXAMPLE

Here is another example of a eight characters chart, which has a strong SELF element. This is the chart of Kenneth, an upwardly mobile Internet executive born in the year of the FIRE SNAKE. Looking at his chart here we can see that his SELF ELEMENT is YANG EARTH sitting on Earth and surrounded by four FIRE elements, which produce earth. Kenneth is also born in the summer when strong FIRE energy strengthens EARTH. So Kenneth is a very strong EARTH person.

Since his SELF-element is strong EARTH, the favourable elements will be those that control and exhaust the earth energy.

This means that the elements that are favourable for Kenneth will be WOOD and METAL, which destroy and exhaust it respectively.

> **It is only when a strong SELF-element is kept under control that the person is able to capture any good fortune that comes his/her way.**

In his case Kenneth's wealth luck is the WATER element but water is missing so there is no obvious indication of wealth luck in his eight characters chart. Kenneth

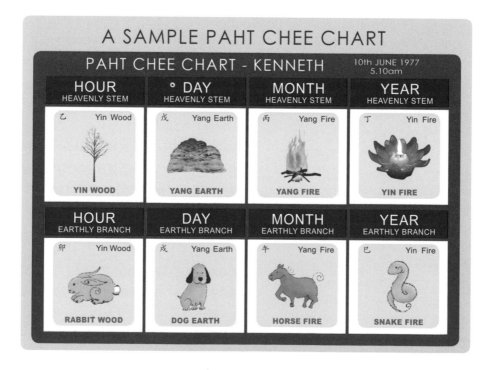

A SAMPLE PAHT CHEE CHART

PAHT CHEE CHART - KENNETH   10th JUNE 1977 5.10am

HOUR HEAVENLY STEM	° DAY HEAVENLY STEM	MONTH HEAVENLY STEM	YEAR HEAVENLY STEM
乙 Yin Wood	戊 Yang Earth	丙 Yang Fire	丁 Yin Fire
YIN WOOD	YANG EARTH	YANG FIRE	YIN FIRE

HOUR EARTHLY BRANCH	DAY EARTHLY BRANCH	MONTH EARTHLY BRANCH	YEAR EARTHLY BRANCH
卯 Yin Wood	戌 Yang Earth	午 Yang Fire	巳 Yin Fire
RABBIT WOOD	DOG EARTH	HORSE FIRE	SNAKE FIRE

has four FIRE elements in his chart and FIRE here stands for his resources. So Kenneth has more than enough to strengthen his EARTH element; this obvious strength causes his chart to be very unbalanced. Kenneth will find his friends becoming his competitors and many will have their own secret agendas that does not bode well for him. During fire years there will emerge competitive pressures that might end up burning Kenneth so he needs to be extra careful during fire years. In this example the year 2006 which is an earth and fire year will not be good for Kenneth. He needs to surround himself with water and metal elements, both of which are missing form his chart. He needs to wear black, blue and white and it will also benefit him to go to the seaside frequently during the year.

At the same time Kenneth has excess EARTH energy, he needs Wood energy in addition to Water and Metal. At home therefore it is a good idea to have plenty of growing live plants. With water and wood surrounding him, Kenneth can successfully bring balance into his private space to overcome the bad luck caused by the elements of the year.

So to recap, Kenneth's chart indicate a woeful lack of the WATER element. There is excess FIRE energy but no WATER. There is also no METAL. That is why Kenneth needs WATER as well as METAL and WOOD to ensure his chart, and therefore his life stays balanced. Having a eight characters chart that is well balanced with all five elements present is an important indicator to having an auspicious life. It is only when the full basket of all five elements is present that good fortune years can manifest good fortune.

Otherwise there will be unexpected obstacles. In this case if the ten-year pillars show that the crucial years of Kenneth's adulthood has the required favourable elements of water and metal then despite the highly imbalanced eight characters chart, Kenneth will enjoy good fortune.

The preceding examples indicate that one simply cannot draw quick conclusions when reading the eight characters. It is the same as reading an Indian Jyotish astrology chart – where the basic chart must be read in conjunction with the Dasars or periods. Chinese and Indian luck prediction always focuses on the periods of one's life. The basic chart offers the eight elements that we are born with, but it is the elements of the periods and of the calendar years and months that, in interacting with the birth elements create powerful influences over one's destiny.

IDENTIFYING FAVOURABLE ELEMENTS

K nowing your SELF ELEMENT, and knowing if it is weak or strong tells you what elements are favourable for you. This relies on the principle of the five elements and their cycles of production and destruction.

Basically the guideline is that when our SELF-element is weak, then we are said to be lacking the Chi of our self-element. We need, and thus will **benefit from being close to, and having the element that produces our element.** This can be reflected in the things we place around us at home, in the office and in the way we dress, put on our make up and also in the way we arrange the spaces in our homes. This is where the eight characters or paht chee chart can have important feng shui implications and far reaching consequences.

In the case of Patrick whose chart is shown here again we have noted that his SELF ELEMENT is WEAK FIRE. In the cycle of elements WOOD produces FIRE. This means immediately that Patrick is a person who will benefit from having wood near him so a tropical type house with lots of plants will benefit him. Patrick will also benefit from anyone whose SELF ELEMENT is WOOD.

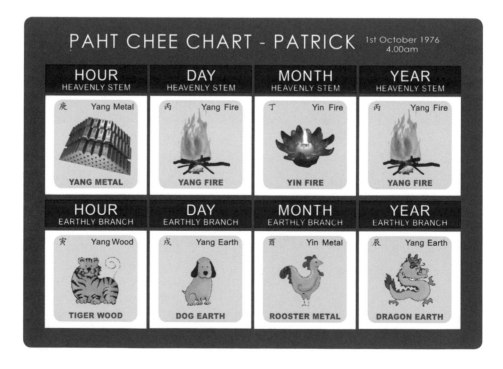

PAHT CHEE CHART - PATRICK   1st October 1976 4.00am

HOUR HEAVENLY STEM	DAY HEAVENLY STEM	MONTH HEAVENLY STEM	YEAR HEAVENLY STEM
庚 Yang Metal	丙 Yang Fire	丁 Yin Fire	丙 Yang Fire
YANG METAL	YANG FIRE	YIN FIRE	YANG FIRE

HOUR EARTHLY BRANCH	DAY EARTHLY BRANCH	MONTH EARTHLY BRANCH	YEAR EARTHLY BRANCH
寅 Yang Wood	戌 Yang Earth	酉 Yin Metal	辰 Yang Earth
TIGER WOOD	DOG EARTH	ROOSTER METAL	DRAGON EARTH

Meanwhile, as an aside, look quickly at the chart and note that if Patrick has a son in later years and his son is a Tiger person, his son will bring excellent good fortune to him, and bring him great joy and happiness. This is because the HOUR PILLAR stands for children.

Anyone amongst Patrick's close circle of friends who are WOOD people will be good for him. Patrick can immediately use this information to check out his girlfriends, his colleagues, his boss, his teachers, his professors, his parents, and his friends to see who amongst them will benefit him the most.

Thus if he is looking for a wife, he should choose a girl who has WOOD as her self-element, or at least be born in a WOOD element year. Such a woman will benefit him and bring him luck. Meanwhile note that while WOOD element people are the most beneficial for him, the second best are people whose self-element is WATER. This is because WATER produces WOOD, and WOOD produces his self-element. Note that in the destructive cycle WATER destroys FIRE but in paht chee analysis, despite that being the case this is the way to identify the second most favourable element. You look for the element that produces the most desirable element. In any case if you look at Patrick's chart you will see that WATER is totally missing from his chart so WATER will be good for him.

Now if Patrick's SELF-element of FIRE had been strong instead of weak, then WOOD would cause him to have too much FIRE, which he does not need. Instead what he needs then would be for his self-element of FIRE to be kept under control, and this would mean that EARTH would be good for him, since EARTH exhausts FIRE.

Knowing his favourable element will enable Patrick to identify his good years; these would be those years that have WOOD as either the heavenly stem or earthly branch. Since his self element is weak FIRE, fire energy is also good for him as this strengthens his FIRE.

Thus I can say that the years 2004 and 2005 would have been good years for Patrick. Why? Because, in these two years, the heavenly stem of the year was WOOD. In 2004 it is JIA Yang WOOD and in 2005 it is YI, Yin WOOD. Since Patrick is a yang fire person the year of the yang wood will be better for him than the year of the yin wood. So 2004 was better for him than 2005. Later we will find when we examine Patrick's Ten year luck pillars that he is going through a pillar which features yang metal and yang water. So the presence of water in his Luck pillar will be helping him. I can thus predict reasonably accurately that 2003 and 2004 were good years for him too.

So Patrick can use information about his favourable elements to check the calendar years, or he can use it to check his ten-year luck pillars, or he can do both. This is the way to identify the ten-year period that will be his stellar years. When WOOD appears in both the ten-year luck pillars and also a calendar year that falls within those ten years that will be the year when Patrick will definitely benefit enormously. That is when he could get a promotion at work, win a big contract, or simply get an offer he cannot refuse.

Most people think it is their animal YEAR of birth that gives them their self-element but as you can see, that is a misconception. If you wish to know what elements are really good for you i.e. to bring you favourable luck, you must first identify your SELF ELEMENT, in your eight characters chart. You also need to determine your unfavourable elements − i.e. those elements that will harm you.

> **The rule is that if your SELF-element is weak, then the element that produces your self-element benefits you. If your self-element is strong, then the element that controls or exhausts it, is beneficial for you. In paht chee the cardinal principle is to ensure there is good balance at all times. Too much or too little of anything constitutes a situation in need of remedy.**

When interpreting the paht chee charts, you need to understand that according to the Chinese everything in the whole Universe is categorized as one of the five elements. There are many attributes and characteristics of wood, fire, earth, metal and water. The more you know what the elements stand for the richer and more in-depth will your analysis be.

Learning how to decipher the paht chee is one thing but accurately interpreting the elements of the eight characters to make luck predictions require experience. Usually the older the person making the reading the more "mature" will be the reading simply because such a person will have 'eaten a lot more salt than most young people have eaten rice". This is an old Chinese proverb that points out the worth of experience.

Here's a tip. Start by taking note first of the general trends of one's life, determining favourable and unfavourable times, years and so forth before going deeper looking for specific answers to specific questions about your love life, your marriage, your children and your potential for work advancement and wealth enhancement. These can all be easily read from the charts but before you enter into those realms of the destiny reading, focus initially on mastering the concept of weak and strong self element and determining favourable and unfavourable elements. Remember that all dimensions of luck prediction that focus on aspirations of wealth and relationships are really relative. Predictions of health are less so. hence a certain amount of subjectivity will always creep into the analysis.

YOUR SELF ELEMENT	Your favourable element is	Your 2nd favourable element is	Your unfavourable element is	Your other unfavourable element is
Weak WOOD	WATER	WOOD	FIRE	METAL
Strong WOOD	METAL	FIRE	WATER	WOOD
Weak FIRE	WOOD	FIRE	EARTH	WATER
Strong FIRE	WATER	EARTH	WOOD	FIRE
Weak EARTH	FIRE	EARTH	METAL	WOOD
Strong EARTH	WOOD	METAL	FIRE	EARTH
Weak METAL	EARTH	METAL	WATER	FIRE
Strong METAL	FIRE	WATER	EARTH	METAL
Weak WATER	METAL	WATER	WOOD	EARTH
Strong WATER	EARTH	WOOD	METAL	WATER

DETERMINING FAVOURABLE & UNFAVOURABLE ELEMENTS

*H*ere is a chart, which tells you generally what your first and second favourable elements are based on your weak or strong SELF ELEMENT.

Use the information here to commit your favourable elements to memory. Pay particular attention to your first favourable element and look out for years when this element occurs either as a heavenly stem or an earthly branch. Those are the years that are good for you. Note however that this rule is a general one and there will be charts where there are exceptions to the rule.

When there are missing elements in your chart for instance, you will need to create balance and to do so, you NEED the missing elements to be present to bring balance to your chart. So the elements in the Table here are based only on the strength and weakness of your SELF element. To have a more accurate diagnosis of favourable and unfavourable elements you may need to also consider other factors.

FINE TUNING FAVOURABLE & UNFAVOURABLE ELEMENTS

*I*t is as important to know what your unfavourable as well as favourable elements are, since the presence of unfavourable elements in the luck pillars or in the calendar years will alert you to the years that will be tiresome and exhausting for you. These will be the years when you should really lie low especially if the astrological charts and your animal sign readings also indicate this.

For instance the year 2006 is a FIRE/EARTH year and thus will prove to be particularly trying for those whose SELF ELEMENT is weak METAL. The FIRE of the heavenly stem of 2006 will send killing Chi to someone whose self element is weak METAL element. However the EARTH element of the branch of the year will strengthen METAL.

The favourable and unfavourable elements have been summarized in a table on page 43 to cover the five elements with a weak or a strong characteristic. Please do study the table carefully since this is a very basic and fundamental part of the eight characters analysis. Later on when we go deeper into the investigation of the ten-year luck pillars, you will need to know your favourable and unfavourable elements.

When studying the chart for signs of wealth potential for instance and trying to analyze one's career luck fame potential or other areas of luck, the favourable elements continue to be a very important input for the reading.

However do note that, it is a good idea to think through the favourable and unfavourable elements in marginal cases where you cannot quite decide if your SELF ELEMENT is weak or strong. It is necessary to study the other elements in the chart and consider the season of the month of birth.

Sometimes there may be a couple of missing elements that make the chart unbalanced and then instead of one or two favourable elements you might well need to make up for the missing elements. In such an instance the missing elements will improve the balance of elements in the eight characters. In another instance a wood person may have been born in winter when it is too cold for the WOOD to survive. Then, WOOD needs heat, and thus will benefit from FIRE even though FIRE exhausts WOOD.

These are factors that require a judgmental input and since every chart is so different, it is not possible to cover all possibilities in a book. The permutations of the eight characters chart are incredibly diverse. This is why one needs to be able to reason things out logically in a comprehensive manner, then only can one get a full reading of the paht chee. However as long as you understand the fundamentals that underpin the theory of the weak or strong SELF ELEMENT you should have little trouble identifying your favourable and unfavourable elements. Determining this correctly is half the battle won.

HELPFUL SUMMARY:

You must identify your SELF ELEMENT, and then determine if it is weak or strong in your chart. When it is weak, your favourable element is the element that produces it. If it is strong your favourable element is one that destroys it. When it is weak, people of similar element are your friends. When it is strong people of similar element become your competitors. Sometimes they even become your enemies. The weaker your self element, the more friends you have; the stronger it is, the more competitors and enemies you will have in your life – i.e. people who will be jealous of you, of your success and your accomplishments.

THE FIVE ELEMENTS & THEIR CYCLES

*I*f you have read this far you will have realized that it is the five elements and their cycles of interaction that unlock the meanings of the paht chee chart and in so doing unlocks the code of our destiny. The Chinese attach extraordinary importance to the five elements - wood, fire, earth, metal, and water. The five elements reflect the cycles of the Universe and links the trinity of existence – heaven, earth and mankind. They exert considerable influence on everyone's personal fortunes. Their significance is related to their cyclical interactions with each other, which may be productive, destructive or exhaustive.

The cycles of interaction provide clues to interpreting life charts. So it is necessary before we go any further, to understand the five elements thoroughly. Generally, when any two elements are in a productive cycle they give rise to harmony, and when any two elements are in a destructive cycle they give rise to conflict.

The productive cycle is where wood burns, producing fire, fire leaves ash producing earth; from earth, metal is formed and mined; then metal melts producing liquid which is viewed as water. Finally water nurtures plants producing wood, after which the cycle starts again. Each element produces the next in a cyclical order. Seeing things in a larger perspective, the productive cycle also reflects Nature's phenomena, and are reflected in the seasons, with each season associated with an element.

The season of growth is spring associated with wood; then comes the heat of summer which is fire. In the middle of the year is earth, which is followed by the season of harvest associated with metal (implements used for harvesting); and finally there is the season of cold associated with water.

In eight characters life prediction, we have seen that the moment of a person's birth can be precisely recorded in terms of the five elements in an eight characters chart. So the year, month, day, and also the hour are expressed as one of the five elements. You can see therefore that the popular method of relying only on the animal sign of the YEAR does not reveal a full picture of a person's destiny. The YEAR animal however sign however offers reliable indications of character and personality attributes, and offers reliable indications of compatibilities with other animals signs.

The fortunes of people based on animal signs follows the astrological methods of determining whether a particular year is good, bad or mediocre. Astrological indications address the immediate fortunes of a person while the eight characters charts take a view of one's entire life destiny. The eight characters chart offers a tantalizing road map to making luck predictions. To interpret the elements however, we need to understand the negative relationships of the elements as well. It is these cycles that will indicate what happens when

the elements exhaust and destroy in their effect on one another.

The exhaustive cycle of the elements is when the relationship causes depleting energy. Thus wood exhausts water; water exhausts metal; metal exhausts earth, earth exhausts fire, and fire exhausts wood. In this cycle the productive cycle reverts backwards. This cycle features prominently in the practice of feng shui as it offers the basis for installing "cures" and "remedies" to overcome feng shui afflictions caused by the passage of time. The exhaustive cure is the productive cycle in reverse. Thus if wood produces fire, then we say that fire exhausts wood. Likewise if water produces wood, then we know that wood exhausts water and so forth.

The destructive cycle is when the combination of elements take on a killing relationship. This is a more severe than the exhaustive cycle.   It happens when water destroys fire; when fire destroys metal, when metal destroys wood, when wood destroys earth, and when earth destroys water. Here the logic is that wood absorbs the goodness and nutrients from the earth and earth sullies the water, which in turn puts out the fire. Then fire reduces metal to liquid from literally melting and destroying it and metal kills wood by chopping trees and plants.

The cycles of the five elements are best committed to memory. This is because you need to know how particular element types might assist or obstruct another. In interpreting the chart, for instance you then know that a predominantly WOOD person would provide sustenance and resources for a FIRE person; or that a FIRE person would stimulate a lazy EARTH person to work and excel.

EARTH types would bring stability to a rash METAL person while a METAL person would make a tranquil and dreamy WATER type person more action oriented. And finally of course a WATER person would provide the sustenance for a WOOD person to grow and expand. Water is good for wood.

Think through what the destructive cycle of the elements would mean for your reading of charts. A WOOD person is certain to drain the resources of an EARTH type person; just as an EARTH person could well destroy a WATER person's life. In the same way a WATER person would likely pour cold water on the FIRE person's enthusiasm and zest for life and a FIRE person would be a formidable enemy of a METAL person. A METAL person would likewise be terribly harmful to a WOOD type person.

There is of course a lot more to follow through. Other factors do come in to either enhance or negate the good and bad influences stated.

This snapshot reading which focuses only on the SELF element is only the tip of the iceberg, interpreting the elements transcends the complete reading of the paht chee, so it is really important for anyone wishing to

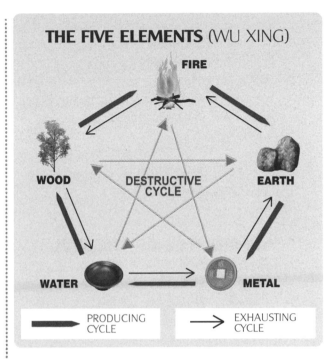

THE FIVE ELEMENTS (WU XING)

FIRE

WOOD

DESTRUCTIVE CYCLE

EARTH

WATER

METAL

PRODUCING CYCLE

EXHAUSTING CYCLE

master the skill of paht chee to know the five elements intimately.

To make it easy, look at the wonderful illustration that summarizes the element cyclical relationship with each other. The outer cycle illustrated as red arrows indicates the productive cycle of the elements. Think of this as a circular flow of energy moving in a positive clockwise direction.

When the energy starts to move in the reverse direction i.e. in an anti clockwise direction, it becomes negative and this is the exhausting cycle. In the illustration it is shown as the blue arrows. The destructive cycle meanwhile, is indicated by the pentacle or five pointed star placed inside. You can see that when you join the elements along this star you have the destructive relationship of the elements. Spend a few moments learning these three cycles thoroughly – it is not difficult since there is common sense logic in the cycles. Note also that the symbolic depiction of the five elements results in a very powerful symbol of western magic and that is the pentacle within a circle. A powerful symbol of protection.

ATTRIBUTES OF THE FIVE ELEMENTS

We turn next to the associated attributes of the five elements. These can be abstract ideas, characteristics or phenomena linked to and associated with each of the elements. Since elements signify everything in the Universe, they represent just about everything in existence! From body parts to compass directions to colours and shapes... here is a non exhaustive tabulation of some attributes that will help you to add depth to your eight characters reading.

Use these as a key to meanings suggested with each element. Pay attention to the seasons and climatic associations as they offer clues to locations, countries and directions especially when the chart suggests a relocation of some kind. Also take note of the feelings associated with the elements. For instance note that the element of fire means joyousness so a person whose self element is fire will likely have a happy disposition. A person whose Self-element is wood tends towards having a quick temper while anyone with water as

GENERAL ATTRIBUTES OF THE FIVE ELEMENTS

ATTRIBUTE	WOOD	FIRE	EARTH	METAL	WATER
MUSICAL NOTE	3E	5G	1C	2D	6A
FEELINGS	ANGER	JOYOUS	COMTEMPLATIVE	SADNESS	FEAR
SEASON	SPRING	SUMMER	4 SEASONS	AUTUMN	WINTER
DIRECTIONS	EAST	SOUTH	CENTER	WEST	NORTH
CLIMATE	WIND	HEAT	WET	DRY	COLD
TASTE	SOUR	BITTER	SWEET	PUNGENT	SALTY
COLOUR	GREEN	RED	YELLOW	WHITE	BLACK

the self element will tend to be conservative, fearful of new experiences and of change. Metal Self element people tend towards sadness while earth element people tend to be philosophers. They are the thinkers of the paht chee chart.

In addition note **colours** associated with each element. These are useful when there is a need to create "balance" in one's chart. Colour therapy based on the five elements is especially useful when you are attempting to enhance your material luck and well-being i.e. this means the luck of career success, marriage happiness and health during old age. If you have determined that fire is your favourable element for instance then wearing red or being surrounded by red will benefit you. If you discovered that water is your unfavourable element then you should avoid wearing black or blue. And so forth...

You can use element therapy to undertake a diagnosis of your element deficiencies and excesses. Chinese healing skills depend on the five elements to aid diagnosis. In traditional Chinese medicine, the ailments of the human body are expressed in terms of either excess or a lack of an identified element. For instance the physician may find the body may have too much heat, too much cold, is too wet or too dry. Or the body could be suffering from wind. Remedies are then recommended on the basis of the elements.

The same logic can be extended to a metaphysical reading of your eight characters. Your luck can be improved and this means that your good luck can be enhanced while bad luck can be reduced or even pressed down simply by using element therapy. Now that you know your self-element you can start using element therapy in your life and see how things begin to get better for you.

In Kung Fu, martial arts moves and in Chi Kung, breathing techniques are expressed as elements. In feng shui the five elements hold the key to unlocking the secrets of the compass directions. In Chinese traditional medicine the healer often uses the taste of bitter to balance out the body perhaps having received too much sugar.

Indeed the Chinese believe that when we ensure the body has a balanced supply of the five tastes symbolizing the five elements – sweet, sour, salty, spicy and bitter – the body will enjoy peak health and one will never be lacking in energy. A great way to maintain this balance within the body is to input five types of vegetables and fruits each day, with each symbolizing one of the five tastes. Try this recipe for a morning smoothie.... green apples (sour); bitter gourd (bitter); star fruit (sweet); capsicum (spicy) and celery (salty). So to unlock the secrets of all the esoteric skills of the Chinese including the paht chee requires knowledge of the five elements.

WEIGHING THE ELEMENTS

Coming back to basics, note that the eight characters chart is interpreted by counting the different elements in the chart. This is referred to as weighing the elements in the chart. This will reveal the "DOMINANT" element and also highlight the missing elements. The dominant element (not the same as the SELF element) is what indicates the personality traits of a person. The strength of these traits is a direct correlation of the frequency or weight of each element in the chart. Before going into the personality reading, let us first look at what to do about missing elements. The eight characters chart shown below reveals a complete absence of WATER so the chart requires water for it to have good balance.

As soon as water is introduced to this person good fortune comes continually. There is also a shortage of FIRE.

The weight of the elements shows 3 metal, 1 fire, 2 wood, 2 earth and zero water. The dominant element of this chart is METAL. At a later stage we will learn what METAL means in this chart but for now let us focus on the overall weighting of elements in the chart. Usually the most auspicious indication is when our "basket of elements" has a balanced weighting of elements – this is when all five elements are present in weightings of 1s, 2s and 3s.

A more or less equal representation of all five elements indicates a well-balanced life where all aspects of creature comforts – health, family, wealth, career, children and so forth will feature in one's life. A balanced basket of elements always suggest a life that is not lacking in any area. This means that the person will enjoy career success, have a good name as well as family happiness and reasonably good health.

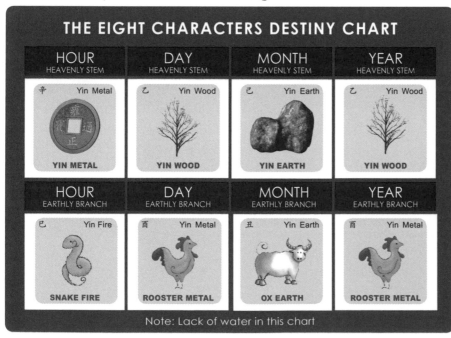

THE EIGHT CHARACTERS DESTINY CHART

HOUR HEAVENLY STEM	DAY HEAVENLY STEM	MONTH HEAVENLY STEM	YEAR HEAVENLY STEM
Yin Metal **YIN METAL**	Yin Wood **YIN WOOD**	Yin Earth **YIN EARTH**	Yin Wood **YIN WOOD**

HOUR EARTHLY BRANCH	DAY EARTHLY BRANCH	MONTH EARTHLY BRANCH	YEAR EARTHLY BRANCH
Yin Fire **SNAKE FIRE**	Yin Metal **ROOSTER METAL**	Yin Earth **OX EARTH**	Yin Metal **ROOSTER METAL**

Note: Lack of water in this chart

If your chart shows a balanced basket of elements you can consider yourself very lucky indeed. When your chart is lacking in one, or even two elements then you should endeavour to compensate for the missing element either by using simple colour therapy in the way you dress or by using feng shui in the way you create your personal space.

In our chart example here the element of water is lacking. This suggests that having a water feature in your home, such as a pool would definitely enhance the chart and bring better all round luck to this person. However note that while water is lacking there are three metals and we know metal produces water. This means the person should have no difficulty in creating the presence of water to benefit his/her life.

REMEDIES FOR MISSING ELEMENTS

Now lets take a look at what happens and what one should do when other elements are missing. For instance, **when wood is lacking** in any chart it is an excellent idea to incorporate wood into the name of the person. This can be words that suggest plants and flowers. Plants symbolize growth while flowers symbolize harvests. The presence of wood in the name of a person where the wood is missing in the eight characters chart immediately brings better fortunes for the person. It is also possible to build a home where there is lavish use of wood.

When the fire element is missing from your eight characters chart, keep your house well lit. Bright lights will benefit you enormously especially if you are also born during the winter months. This means you need the warmth of summer. Also incorporate fire element words into your name. These include words like the sun, sunshine, brightness and so forth. **If the metal element** is missing from your eight characters chart, introduce lots of metallic energy into your space. Wear plenty of fine jewellery especially ornaments made of gold. Incorporate the word 'gold" in your name. You can observe for instance the word Kim is very popular with the Chinese — this is the word for gold and it also is the Chinese word for metal.

Finally **if earth is the missing element** in your chart, let stones, crystals and earth materials dominate your space. Also incorporate earth words into your name - here it is a good idea to use words that mean precious stones - diamonds, ruby and so forth. The Chinese are also very fond of using precious stones and especially the word jade to name their children. When there is more than one element missing either choose only the missing element that corresponds to your favourable elements only OR incorporate both the missing elements into your name. Remember to maintain a balance of elements at all times. Refrain from overdoing. When a single element dominates the whole chart gets unbalanced — that is when obstacles will develop to bring you some pretty nasty aggravations.

HIDDEN ELEMENTS IN THE PAHT CHEE CHART

*T*he paht chee chart is made up of eight characters, and hence its name. The words paht chee is a literal translation of eight characters. The chart however shows only the visible elements. The chart also has hidden elements and for a more accurate weighting of the dominant elements of the chart, and also for a more complete reading of destiny & personality traits, we must also look for hidden elements in the chart. Hidden elements are present when the stems and branches in the chart manifest certain combinations. There can be hidden heavenly stems or hidden earthly branches. We should look for these hidden elements and then see if these elements are favourable; whether they support or clash with the other elements in the chart. Hidden elements will add to the basket of elements and these can either create a better balance and hence a better life for the person. Or the hidden elements could be harmful or cause excessive dominance of certain elements thereby creating obstacles to success.

LOOKING FOR HIDDEN HEAVENLY STEM ELEMENTS

*I*n the eight characters chart the top four characters are heavenly stems. We look for hidden elements by studying the elements of the four stems. First take note that heavenly stems produce a hidden element when a Yang stem combines with a Yin stem. The hidden element created is a new element. Thus:

- *When yang wood combines with yin earth the hidden element is* **earth**
- *When yin wood combines with yang metal the hidden element is* **metal**
- *When yang fire combines with yin metal the hidden element created is* **water**
- *When yin fire combines with yang water the hidden element created is* **wood**
- *When yang earth combines with yin water the hidden element created is* **fire**

When hidden heavenly stems get created in your chart it is usually read as a good sign and if the element created are favourable for you and improves the overall balance of the chart it is exceptionally good. Look at the example chart shown below. Note that all the heavenly stems here are yin so there are no hidden elements in this chart. Take note that hidden elements can occur only when the pillars have both yin and yang heavenly stems in the chart.

EXAMPLE CHART	HOUR	DAY	MONTH	YEAR
Heavenly Stem Element	YIN METAL	YIN WOOD	YIN EARTH	YIN WOOD
Earthly Branch Element	YIN SNAKE	YIN ROOSTER	YIN OX	YIN ROOSTER

HOW TO LOOK FOR HIDDEN EARTHLY BRANCH ELEMENTS

Next we examine the earthly branches and investigate whether there are any hidden elements amongst the branches. These are the four elements shown in the bottom row of the eight characters chart.

In the case of the earthly branches, hidden (i.e. new) elements manifest in two ways, firstly with the combination of three branches and secondly through combinations of two branches. When hidden elements emerge as a result of three branches combining, the new hidden element created is much stronger than when it is the result of two branches combining.

THERE ARE FOUR THREE-BRANCH COMBINATIONS

These are the combinations of the allies among the 12 animal signs:

1. When Monkey, Rat & Dragon combine a new element of **water** is created

2. When Pig, Rabbit & Sheep combine a new element of **wood** is created

3. When Snake, Rooster & Ox combine a new element of **metal** is created

4. When Tiger, Horse & Dog combine a new element of **fire** is created

THERE ARE SIX TWO BRANCH COMBINATIONS

These are combinations of the secret friends amongst the 12 animal signs:

Rat (water) combining with Ox (earth) creates hidden **earth**

Tiger (wood) combining with Pig (water) creates hidden **wood**

Rabbit (wood) combining with Dog (earth) creates hidden **fire**

Dragon (earth) combining with Rooster (metal) creates hidden **metal**

Snake (fire) combining with Monkey (metal) creates hidden **water**

Horse (fire) combining with Sheep (earth) creates hidden **fire**

EXAMPLE CHART	HOUR	DAY	MONTH	YEAR
Heavenly Stem Element	YIN METAL	YANG WOOD	YIN EARTH	YIN WOOD
Earthly Branch Element	YIN FIRE SNAKE*	YIN METAL MONKEY*	YIN EARTH OX	YIN METAL ROOSTER

Look at the example chart above and note that the animals in the four pillars show that two separate hidden elements have been created:

First is when Snake, Rooster & Ox combine to create the hidden element of **metal**.

Second is when Snake combines with Monkey to create a hidden element of **water**.

Note also that this chart lacks water so with the presence of hidden water the chart is strengthened. Also note that in this chart, the self-element is weak wood. So the hidden water strengthens it. The hidden metal also creates water so that is excellent. But the hidden metal harms the wood. So of the two hidden elements, water is more beneficial and metal is more powerful. Overall however with the presence of water the chart is made instantly more balanced, and therefore better. This indicates this person can overcome obstacles. What it needs would be plenty of water and wood to enhance his/her life.

When hidden elements reveal the presence of favourable elements they indicate unexpected support, a windfall or it can indicate marriage or children, which appears missing in the original eight characters chart. Check what the hidden element means in your chart and extend the reading accordingly.

Remember there can be hidden elements created by the stems as well as by the branches and hidden elements are very powerful.

With the addition of hidden elements you have a new basket of elements and you can see if there are still elements that are "missing". If so you should endeavour to balance them out.

At the same time also be on the look out for "overweight" elements. Generally, out of twelve elements, if all the elements are present and averaging two or three, the chart is said to be very well balanced. And if there is zero of any element then the element is missing. When you have four of any element then that is said to be a very dominant element. When there is more than four then the element is said to be in excess. When the dominant element stands for wealth it means there is a big likelihood of this person getting rich and prosperous but for this prosperity to manifest the self-element must be made strong.

I hope that you getting a feel for the way eight characters charts are read. Everything revolves around the relationship of the five elements as well as on the weighting of the different elements. If you are reading about eight characters for the first time it might seem a little confusing but after reading one or two sample charts you will start to get a very good idea of the information that is being revealed by the charts. So hang in there and be patient. There are more exciting revelations to come!

PERSONALITY & CHARACTER TRAITS

How do you respond to challenges and opportunities? What are your underlying tendencies and what kind of people do you have affinity with? While your horoscope animal sign (the earthly branch of the YEAR pillar) will give you a good idea of the kind of person you are based on the astrological readings of your sign, it is your basket of elements that will reveal how you are most likely to respond to the opportunities and challenges that come into your life. For this you need to weigh the elements in your chart to identify your dominant elements. The chart is what identifies the potential of your destiny, revealing what you are capable of when you are at your best and when you are able to rise above obstacles caused by any number of annual, astrological or feng shui afflictions.

The eight characters chart tells you much about yourself by highlighting shortcomings (lack of certain elements) that block you from making the most of opportunities. It can be that you are naturally fearful of taking risks and so you will need to strengthen your courage and your vitality; or perhaps it is due to your over aggressive nature that can rub people up the wrong way thereby losing you the main chance; here maybe you have excess of some dominant element that could be making you come across too aggressive and too strong.

So here you will need an element to suppress over exuberance. Knowing your own latent weakness, as expressed in the chart, will go a long way towards ensuring that you benefit more from the opportunities that come your way.

The Chinese believe it is not enough to be going through a good ten-year luck cycle or be visited with good luck chi forces. That is the heaven luck in our destiny. Earth luck is when we are able to recognize the opportunity when it comes. But there is also the input of our own actions, our attitudes and our responses to the big breaks that appear in our life. If we do not respond in a way that will maximize our good fortune, it becomes wasted. Similarly if we allow our own arrogance or dogmatism to spoil our chances for success, we will have no one to blame but ourselves.

It is from this perspective that understanding our own character and personality traits can be such a boon in helping us make better use of the resources and opportunities that come into our life. It also transforms our attitudes, making us into better, nicer people as well.

How we respond to opportunities and lucky breaks is a function of many factors. Thus while different types of luck can act as catalysts for us to move to the next stage of our life, whether the next stage is more successful or happier depends on how we respond to the catalyst. This should be the reason for making the personality reading as revealed by the basket of elements. So the weighting exercise becomes important as it reveals the strength of the different elements in our basket.

When an element is completely missing from your chart, you can ignore the personality reading associated with that element but you must still try to reduce the "imbalance" by surrounding yourself with people and objects that are strongly associated with the missing element. Simply by doing this, you will have enhanced your chances for happiness and success and improved your luck.

WEIGHTING THE ELEMENTS

When you have become more sensitive to the weighting of elements you can fine-tune the interaction of elements that surround you. Note that all five elements have a role to play in your well-being. The key is how we use their weighting to obtain the maximum benefit.

The selection of elements is a dynamic process, changing with the season and the year. So what is "beneficial" for you is as much a function of your chart, and its basket of elements, as it is on the element that is ruling the season and the year you are going through. For instance if water is beneficial for you in that you lack water then the season of winter is better for you then the season of summer, and hence during winter you will need less of water. Likewise if fire is beneficial for you, you will need more of it in winter than in summer.

To make a character reading of your basket of elements, note that as a general rule of thumb, a weighting of 4 indicates strength as well as a positive outcome from possessing the characteristic indicated by the element. But when the weighting exceeds four, the strong point transforms into a liability. Excess of any element always creates a negative result. Remember this in all aspects of paht chee reading.

Personality readings based on the five elements are summarized as follows. Before reading this section make sure you have the weighting of your basket of elements in front of you.

WOOD 木

A high wood weighting indicates a strongly creative person. This is a person who has amazing far sightedness and vision, and is also artistic, possessing vivid powers of imagination. This is someone who strives strongly for the stars, someone whose ambitions may over reach his/her ability. A high weighting is suggested if there are four of the wood element in the chart. If you have a high weighting of wood it is likely that you will grab at opportunities that come your way and you will react in an imaginative and creative way that will benefit you.

If you have a weighting of more than 4, then you might just be over reaching. Your ambition may get the better of you. Be careful, be courageous but do not ever be rash. Never allow your creativity to descend into obsessive ness, for then you will miss the wood for the trees. Your vision could get clouded when it really should be sharp with crystal clarity.

Someone with a two or a three weighting would demonstrate creativity and artistic leanings yet have the right amount of practical attitude to stay stable and balanced. Reaction to opportunities will be more measured and well thought out. This is because with a rating of 2 or 3 the person is also benefiting from inputs form other elements.

If the chart is missing the wood element altogether or has only one, it indicates a lack of creativity and imagination. Such people tend to have little time for the grand vision and tend to be impatient with dreamers. They will seldom be able to take advantage of opportunities that come their way. Such a waste of course. If this describe you, try surrounding yourself with some water element friends, or simply have water near you – water will help overcome inertia and make you more alert to the big breaks that come your way.

FIRE 火

A high fire weighting indicates a very extravagant and vivacious personality, someone who stimulates others and inspires those around them to follow suit. A high weighting of fire suggests a person who is usually very charismatic, has loads of energy and vitality and is also highly intelligent, sharp and incisive. Here is someone to be reckoned with, someone whose smartness could degenerate into an over bearing attitude that put people off.

When opportunity knocks, fire dominant people will usually respond with the grand gesture. They allow their mind to expand exponentially and when they do succeed, it will be in a blaze of publicity. They will dazzle in the limelight and their star will shine brightly. When the weighting goes beyond a 4, the fire element will burn itself out. A two or a three weighting suggests someone highly spirited and active and such people usually respond enthusiastically but there will be a steadying influence provided by some other element as well, so their response is usually rather more careful. They will generally therefore make good use of opportunities that come their way.

A zero or a one weighting indicates a quiet homely personality. They will usually be blind to the main chance, being rather obtuse or naïve and this will cause them to miss out when opportunities come It is as if they wear blinkers. So do note that merely having the indication of good fortune is not enough. You also need to possess the sharpness of character to see, the attitude to respond and the courage to take action – each in correct measure – to really benefit from good fortune that comes your way.

EARTH 土

A high earth weighting indicates someone determined to the point of being obstinate and dogmatic. Earth is usually associated with stability and someone very circumspect and proper. You will seldom find an earth person being the live wire of any party. Usually he/she will resonate with the grounding stability of earth. So when opportunity knocks the response from a dominant earth person is almost certain to be planned, calculated and most importantly lead to success. Sometimes however when the response is too measured and too well planned, the opportunity could slip through one's fingers.

When the weighting goes beyond four and there is an excess of earth, success potential definitely turns into a loss situation. Here the excess earth causes a plodding response which translates into "losing the main chance".

A two or three weighting of earth indicates a practical down to earth person, who is also reliable, and trustworthy. When helped by the presence of fire element in equal measure an earth person will make a great deal of the opportunity that comes into the life chart. This kind of person will almost benefit from a good luck period and will not lose out any big break that comes his/her way.

If the weighting of earth is one or zero it suggests someone who is definitely less grounded, probably rash and perhaps unreliable. In fact if the earth element is completely missing some experts see this as indicating a tendency to dishonesty. This is useful knowledge for human resources manager to take note of when hiring employees!

METAL 金

A high weighting of the metal element is a clear indication of someone lacking in sentiments and emotions, at least publicly. Such people tend to be shy and they cover their shyness with a brusque manner. They are comfortable in situations that do not require any show of emotion. Corporate situations benefit these types as they can safely hide behind their corporate titles, pin striped suits and office positions.

Such people are usually very competitive, very entrepreneurial, very business-like and aggressively direct in dealings with others. They are extremely enterprising individuals and can be relied upon to get the work done. They also tend to be courageous and are the stuff of heroes. When they enter into a period of good luck, such people are literally unstoppable. They will benefit from the main chance unless their weighting goes beyond four, and then there is the danger of there being a surplus of aggression. Deals can fall through then and success is blocked by a dogmatism that proves negative.

A two or three weighting indicates possession of the same positive qualities but in smaller measure, and thus more amenable to success. If you have a two or three rating of metal, you are probably a sporting individuals who is competitive but also astute. Sp you know when to be obstinate and when to give in.

When metal element is totally lacking in the chart the person will demonstrate a lack of will. There is little discipline in such a person's life. There is a tendency towards being sentimental and indecisive.

WATER 水

A high weighting in the water element indicates a gifted intellectual. Here is a person who has amazing communicative, research and scholarly skills. This is a person who is eloquent and adventurous with a tendency to be effusive and spontaneously loud dealing with others. They will take easily to success opportunities. If there is a surplus or excess of water, they could waste their good fortune away through lack of focused motivation and probably also an inability to recognize their own aspirations.

Those with a two or three rating are talkative, bright and lucid. Since intelligence is highly indicated by the water element, such people will definitely recognize opportunities that materialize for them, and they will have no problem getting used to better lifestyles and enjoying their success. Those with a zero weighting or with just a single water element in their chart tend to be secretive and shy. They are cautious in business and reserved socially. They will waffle along and lose sight of opportunities.

> **NOTE:**
> **Here's a tip when making a personality reading. Use the meanings given here to read the element indicated in the DAY heavenly stem. This is your SELF-element and it offers strong indications of personality and your character traits. It also indicates strong and weak points and reveals the way you respond to opportunities.**

In reading the summary bear in mind that most people demonstrate a mixture of two or three traits in different proportions. And there will usually be one or two missing elements. It is not possible to offer a complete recipe approach to reading the paht chee since different combinations of the elements could give rise to confusion. There will be instances when you must use your judgment whether to put greater weight for one element over another.

When in doubt you can also look to the elements prevailing in any year to give you extra leads to the reading.

Part Three

FIVE TYPES OF LUCK

WEALTH, FRIENDSHIPS, POWER, INTELLIGENCE & RESOURCES

FIVE TYPES OF LUCK

ooking for Wealth, Friendships, Power, Intelligence & Resources in your chart. The eight characters chart is a reliable indicator of the five basic kinds of luck that determine the material quality of our lifestyle. These luck categories represent the sum total of most people's aspirations, and these are the things that everyone wants to find out when they arrange to have their future read. Paht chee offers an easy way of determing how much happiness and success potential is revealed in the charts.

1 WEALTH & FINANCIAL SUCCESS

For example, everyone, including you the reader, wants to know if you have the destiny to become rich, and if so at what age it will start to happen i.e. when the money will actually come "rolling in". Many also want to know exactly how rich they will be?

How does the wealth come about – through your own efforts, your intelligence and creativity; or through making a brilliant marriage or through the help and patronage of someone, a relative, a boss or a powerful mentor perhaps? In eight characters reading wealth is divided into two kinds and these are **direct wealth** and **unexpected wealth**.

How long do you have to wait and what signs can there be to indicate when you are about to strike it big? There are so many questions we have in our heads relating to this ONE type of luck alone. Getting reasonably rich is something most of us aspire to and the good

**WEALTH IS SIGNIFIED BY THE ELEMENT
THAT IS DESTROYED BY THE SELF ELEMENT**

so if SELF is WOOD, WEALTH luck is EARTH

so if SELF is WATER, WEALTH luck is FIRE

so if SELF is METAL, WEALTH luck is WOOD

so if SELF is EARTH, WEALTH luck is WATER

so if SELF is FIRE, WEALTH luck is METAL

thing about paht chee is that besides revealing the likelihood of wealth in our charts, implicit in the analysis are remedies and cures related to the five elements that we can put into place to "help the wealth luck along". Indeed this is the aspect of eight characters that is the most exciting − that we can indeed give our wealth luck a boost.

To find out if you have wealth in your chart, you must first determine if the element, which represents wealth to you, is present in your chart. From the illustration here, note that **WEALTH in anyone's chart is signified by the element that is destroyed by the self-element.** So if your self-element is Wood, then since it destroys earth, earth element signifies wealth in your chart and your luck pillars. It is a good idea to commit this formula to memory as it helps you to develop an easy familiarity with the five elements.

If the wealth element is present in your eight characters chart, the next step is to find out how many times the wealth element occurs. When your wealth element occurs 1, 2 or 3 times it indicates the potential for wealth luck, but note this only indicates the **potential** for wealth, the first step. When the wealth element can be found in the chart the potential for you being rich is there. Sometimes when the wealth element is missing, it can show up as a hidden element. This sometimes suggests there is hidden wealth in your chart and it is regarded as a very auspicious indication indeed.

You can also have too much of the wealth element. Thus, for instance if say, Wood is your wealth element and you have four or five Wood in your chart, then from being a positive indication it becomes something negative since this is regarded as excessive. Then far from being an indication of you becoming wealth and rich it can indicate your obsession with getting rich to an extent that it will harm you. The remedy is to introduce the element that exhausts the wealth element with the intention of weakening it.

The second step is to determine whether the wealth elements that appear in your chart are yin or yang. This is described as the gender of the element. When the wealth element and the self element are both yin or both yang then the wealth is unexpected wealth. When one is yin and the other is yang then the wealth is direct wealth. In your chart you can have both kinds of wealth.

2 FRIENDS, FOES & COMPETITORS

The chart can also tell you a great deal about the relationships you have with the people your life touches - relatives, colleagues and friends who may be your allies or they may be your competitors. Indeed the broad category of "friends" is lumped under the element that is the same as the SELF element.

Note that friends can bring negative or positive luck into your life. How friends relate and interact with you is determined by whether your self-element is weak or strong. When the SELF-element is weak then each time the same element occurs in your chart, it means there are good positive friends coming in to support you;

> FRIENDS ARE SIGNIFIED
> BY THE ELEMENT
> THAT IS THE SAME AS
> THE SELF ELEMENT
>
> * IF THE SELF IS WEAK,
> FRIENDS WILL HELP IF THE
> SELF IS STRONG, FRIENDS
> BECOME COMPETITIVE

If your SELF element is strong however, then each time it is repeated in the chart, the element will generally signify enemies and competitors, people who could well do you in and betray you. In modern scenarios, this aptly describes politics and power play at the office. If you look within your own life you will realize that to some of you, friends are always there to help you, bring you comfort and assistance when you need it. To others, friends can maybe stab them in the back, set themselves up as competitors and generally cause grief and heartache in their life.

In short friends can be enemies as well. To discover what your destiny holds in store for you regarding friends, you can look at your eight characters chart to see if yours is a life blessed with many good friends or whether yours is a life where you always need to watch your back and where friends are always seeming to compete with you, practicing one up-manship at every possible moment.

3 POWER, RANK, RECOGNITION

Whether or not you are destined to be publicly lauded, honoured, hold high positions and be the recipient of VIP titles is determined by the presence of the element that symbolizes such recognition in the chart. POWER and rank are symbolized by the element that destroys your SELF element.

Thus when your self element is WOOD then in your chart you must look for stems and branches that are Metal if power, titles and rank is what you want in life. Again if the power element is present either singly or as 2 or 3 it is an excellent indication that you will attain high recognition in life.

More than that however is a cause for caution to be exercised since it means you have too many of the Power elements. In this case you might need to introduce an element that exhausts the excessive Power element. Note that while some of you may say you do not want or need Power luck, in truth all of us do.

POWER IS SIGNIFIED BY THE ELEMENT THAT DESTROYS THE SELF ELEMENT

so if SELF is FIRE, POWER luck is WATER

if SELF is WATER, POWER luck is EARTH

if SELF is EARTH, POWER luck is WOOD

if SELF is METAL, then POWER luck is FIRE

if SELF is WOOD, POWER luck is METAL

Unless we have a certain amount of control luck, which comes with having power and influence, it is hard to get things done and even more difficult to live without aggravations. Having Power luck does not refer to political type power. Instead it refers to how influential and highly respected one is. Usually when the head of the house has this luck, and he activates it with a Ru Yi, placed behind him at work, then it can safely be said that he will be unbeatable.

4 INTELLIGENCE & CREATIVITY

This is the luck, which is considered to be the most significant and important to have. In the eight characters chart it is signified by the element that is produced by the SELF element.

Example: If your self-element is water, then since water produces wood, it is the wood element, which symbolize your intelligence and creativity in your chart. You can check the your Intelligence element from the illustration here. It is important that there is at least one such element in the eight characters since a total absence of it often indicates someone who is mentally challenged UNLESS it occurs as a hidden element either as a stem or a branch arising from the combination of any two of the stems and branches in the chart. (read section on hidden elements). The presence of the intelligence element is also seen as a powerful antidote to the absence of other luck elements.

For example even if you do not have the wealth element present in your chart, by having the Intelligence element present, this suggests you might indeed be able to make good money during years when the wealth element appears in your luck pillars. Indeed I have seen the eight characters charts of people whose chart showed a superficial lack of their wealth element amongst the basic eight characters but instead had three of the elements that indicate intelligence.

INTELLIGENCE IS SIGNIFIED BY THE ELEMENT THAT IS PRODUCED BY THE SELF ELEMENT

so if the SELF is WOOD,
INTELLIGENCE is FIRE

if the SELF is WATER,
INTELLIGENCE is WOOD

if the SELF is EARTH,
INTELLIGENCE is METAL

if the SELF is FIRE,
INTELLIGENCE is EARTH

if the SELF is METAL,
INTELLIGENCE is WATER

Then when I examined further I would discover at least one hidden wealth element. With just this single wealth indicator this person used his great store of intelligence luck to carve out a great fortune. What was very interesting is that usually such people make their fortunes during years when the wealth element makes an appearance in the luck pillars or the calendar years.

The eight characters interpretation always acknowledges the vital influence of one's own creative mind and one's intelligence and common sense. Note that this, together with the element that spells resources are the most important elements that should be present in one's chart.

Should there be an excess of the intelligence element however, then the indication is mental instability. Just as the West recognizes genius as bordering on insanity likewise when there is too many of the elements that indicate intelligence in the chart, the indications have turned negative.

5 RESOURCES, SUPPORT & AUTHORITY

The fifth kind of luck revealed by the elements in the chart is that of resources and support. The element that shows whether one has enough resources and strength to manifest all the goodies indicated in the chart is the element that produces the SELF-element. So if the self-element is Earth, then fire, which produces earth indicates one's resources.

RESOURCES IS SIGNIFIED BY THE ELEMENT THAT PRODUCES THE SELF ELEMENT

so if SELF is FIRE,
RESOURCES luck is WOOD

if SELF is WOOD,
RESOURCES luck is WATER

if SELF is EARTH,
RESOURCES luck is FIRE

if SELF is METAL,
RESOURCES luck is EARTH

if SELF is WATER,
RESOURCES luck is METAL

Many experts on eight characters hold the view that without sufficient resources it is simply impossible for any kind of good luck to manifest into our lives.

For instance no matter how much wealth or recognition luck may seem to be present in the eight characters chart, unless the chart also has elements that signify our resources, all other kinds of good luck indicated simply will not materialize.

It is like saying "I almost had it" or that "I came this close to getting it". Well folks a miss is as good as a mile. The good news is that eight characters does prescribe cures that make up for vital missing elements. So a lack of resources can always be "artificially" created either by placing it in our names, or by ensuring a good amount of it is present in our living environment. Some experts maintain that when the resources luck is missing and the self element is weak, it suggests poor health and a life of suffering.

FOUR PILLARS

HOUR	DAY	MONTH	YEAR
丁 Yin Fire	己 Yin Earth	庚 Yin Metal	己 Yin Earth
乙卯 Yin Wood Rabbit	癸亥 Yin Water Boar	丙午 Yang Fire Horse	丁巳 Yin Fire Snake

午未申酉戌亥
子丑寅卯辰巳

EIGHT LUCK PILLARS

1	11	21	31	41	51	61	71
己 Yin Earth	戊 Yang Earth	丁 Yin Fire	丙 Yang Fire	乙 Yin Wood	甲 Yang Wood	癸 Yin Water	壬 Yang Water
巳 Yin Fire Snake	辰 Yang Earth Dragon	卯 Yin Wood Rabbit	寅 Yang Wood Tiger	丑 Yin Earth Ox	子 Yang Water Rat	亥 Yin Water Boar	戌 Yang Earth Dog

Element	Areas of Life
METAL	Inteligence, Creativity
EARTH	Friends, Foe, Colleagues, Competition
WOOD	Recognition, Power, Rank
FIRE	Resource, Support, Authority
WATER	Wealth, Financial Success

THE TIMING OF LUCK

So altogether the eight characters chart reveals five major types of PROSPECTIVE LUCK that relate to wealth, friendships, power, intelligence and resources. Since the potential for each of these five types of luck is revealed via the elements, part of the eight characters reading focuses on finding these elements and then determining when the luck indicated will manifest into our lives. This is where the significance of timing enters the picture. To determine timing we look at the elements of the ten year luck pillars and also the elements of every calendar year.

> NOTE:
> The five elements that symbolize the five kinds of luck are identified in your four pillars charts that you can download and print out from www.wofs.com.

Once you know how to identify the presence of different kinds of luck from your chart, you can proceed to undertake a detailed analysis of your luck potential – looking at both the eight characters as well as the ten year luck pillars.

CAN I BECOME A MILLIONAIRE?

At what age can I make my first million? Where will my wealth come from?

Signs of wealth in your eight characters chart are indicated by the presence of the element that represents WEALTH in your chart. So the first step to finding out if you have the destiny to be rich is to identify the element that signifies WEALTH luck in your chart. The table below indicates what the WEALTH element is, based on your SELF-element.

Now look at your own paht chee chart and count the number of times your Wealth element appears in your eight characters. If your WEALTH element is missing it means you do not possess any **obvious** wealth luck. It is

If your self element is...	WOOD	WATER	METAL	EARTH	FIRE
Your wealth element is...	EARTH	FIRE	WOOD	WATER	METAL

probably difficult for there to be direct wealth in your destiny. But this does not mean you will be poor. Not having the wealth element does not mean having no income. But it does mean that you are unlikely to have your own business or possess a great deal of asset wealth or be able to accumulate very much in terms of property. It will be difficult for you become seriously wealthy.

If your WEALTH element does appear in your chart, count the number of times it appears taking note that the best is for it to appear 2 or 3 times. Anything more can be excessive and when it is excessive, instead of indicating wealth, it merely suggests that in your life, you are likely to be near to wealth, or be near wealthy people, but you do not own nor control the wealth. So it can suggest a career in banking or working for a very rich man but it does not necessarily suggest that you yourself will become wealthy.

Sometimes having the WEALTH element appear too many times can indicate loss of wealth, or it may be suggesting that pursuing WEALTH can be the cause of your downfall. In eight characters whenever there is excess, indications of good fortune transform into misfortune. In such instances you must place antidotes in position. Use the element that exhausts the wealth element in the space around you. e.g. if your wealth element is wood and there is too much wood in your chart place bright lights near you and wear lots of red to exhaust the wood energy.

Having said that, if your WEALTH element appears 3 or even 4 times in your chart, it does suggest strongly there is WEALTH potential in your life. You have the destiny to become a millionaire, and probably even a multi millionaire, but for this to happen and for you to make serious money, you need to tone down the wealth element and more importantly, you need to be strong enough (ie have the resources and support for your self element) for the wealth luck to materialize.

This means you need to look at how the SELF element is doing. For instance if your SELF element is weak, then to benefit from any WEALTH luck that appears in your chart, your SELF element needs to be sustained and strengthened.

This usually happens:
1. **when you encounter your favourable nourishing element in a calendar year OR**

2. **when you encounter your favourable nourishing element in your ten year luck pillar OR**

3. **when your surroundings (your home and office) are dominated by the presence of your nourishing element, OR**

4. **a combination of all three of the above.**

EXAMPLE 1:

If your SELF-element is WEAK WOOD, you will need WATER before your wealth luck of EARTH can manifest. What this means is that the most likely time for your wealth luck to ripen so that you get rich, is during a ten-year luck pillar that has WATER in it. It can also happen during calendar years when the WATER element is present. It is even better during calendar years having both WATER and EARTH.

In your case, because your self-element is weak wood, you cannot get rich when there is a shortage of water. During calendar years when either FIRE or METAL is present, your WOOD is weakened even more — so those years do not benefit you, and in fact those years are simply not good for you. If EARTH is present but is combined with FIRE or METAL, you will not be strong enough to benefit from your WEALTH luck brought by the earth element. In such years surrounding yourself with WATER (e.g. wearing blue or having water features near you) will definitely improve your WEALTH luck. The best then is to have a swimming pool and to immerse yourself in water everyday.

So if weak wood is your self-element, the years 2004 and 2005, being wood/metal years were of less benefit to you and were unlikely to be serious wealth accumulation years. These were years when you will have problems but you will have friends coming to your aid. This is because the wood in these years represents friends in your chart. In 2006 there is fire and earth so there is wealth luck waiting to manifest; but there is also a great deal of exhaustion caused by the fire. If you have water near by then you are sure to benefit from the earth element. If you lack water, then wealth cannot manifest.

EXAMPLE 2:

If your SELF-element is STRONG METAL, your WEALTH element is WOOD. Here because your self-element is strong, your wealth luck when it appears can overwhelm you and your arrogance will block the wealth from manifesting, unless your strength is lessened. So even when your eight characters chart shows 3 to 4 times appearance of WOOD i.e. your WEALTH element, your wealth luck will only manifest during the ten year luck pillar where there is the presence of fire or water or both. These are the elements that will keep your strong metal under control thereby enabling you to benefit from your wealth luck. The best calendar years are those years when there is the presence of both fire with wood, or water with wood.

So if strong metal is your self-element, the years 2004/2005 are not years when your wealth luck will materialize either. The elements of these two years are wood and metal. There is money to be made and you will see the opportunities but you are unable to control your strength sufficiently for the money luck to manifest — this is because your self-element is too strong. There will be competitors who will spoil things for you. This is because when your self-element is strong, then when your element makes an appearance instead of signifying friends they signify competitors. So in 2004/2005 the metal earthly branch brought you competitors. In 2006 the year's elements are fire and earth so it is at best a neutral year for a person whose self element is strong metal.

LOOK AT YOUR TEN-YEAR LUCK PILLARS

*T*o determine the timing of luck arrival, or to identify the good and bad periods of one's life, it is necessary to look at the luck pillars that come with your eight characters chart and from the ten year luck pillars search for a pillar that has your most favourable element or elements present.

As you have learnt from the previous chapter, your favourable element depends on your SELF-element and on whether it is weak or strong. It is during the ten-year luck period when your favourable element appears either as the earthly branch or as the heavenly stem that your luck during that ten-year period will be good enough to trigger the ripening of your wealth luck. If it appears as the heavenly stem, wealth luck manifests during the first five years and if it is your earthly branch then wealth luck gets activated during the second five years of your ten-year luck pillar. When both the stem and branch are your favourable elements your luck is great because you will have a run of ten auspicious years when you will accumulate great wealth.

Note however that when the WEALTH element is present in your eight characters chart it does not always suggest wealth. We must also look at the weighting. If you have only a single wealth element, it is not sufficient to bring you much wealth. When there is a weighting of 2 to 3 however it is good indication of strong wealth luck. Usually having 3 of the WEALTH element is sufficient to indicate pretty serious wealth but we must also look at the ten-year luck pillars to see if you also have the auspicious pillars necessary to cause your WEALTH luck element to ripen into reality. If you have any hidden elements either as heavenly stems or earthly branches, and these signify wealth luck then your wealth will come to you from unexpected quarters. Do take note that hidden wealth luck elements are very strong indicators of wealth potential.

If you do find an auspicious ten year luck pillar in your chart and there are also WEALTH luck elements present in your eight characters chart in good numbers, then you can be reasonably confident that there is definitively wealth in your destiny. You can be sure then that you will become rich, even seriously wealthy.

CALENDAR YEARS

We also need to look at the calendar years and check its respective heavenly stem and earthly branch elements – the elements of any current year will either strengthen or weaken the elements of your luck pillar. They will also impact on the SELF-element.

Remember that the SELF must be strong (but not too strong) to benefit from any kind of luck and this includes wealth luck. There are eight characters experts who place such heavy weighting on the influence of the calendar years that they believe wealth luck or any kind of luck for that matter, will simply not actualize when the elements of the year hurt the SELF-element.

This is the dynamic of eight characters reading. It suggests that we will always need to take account of the elements that are ruling during any given year. It also suggests that the ruling elements of even the MONTH and DAY will impact on the SELF-element thereby having a bearing on one's luck in that month or day.

NOTE:

This is the method that Chinese luck prediction merchants use to calculate the truly brilliant days of the year for anyone. The ruling elements of the YEAR are too important to ignore, although of course, out of expediency, many of us ignore the MONTH and the DAY elements. However for those of you who wish to do so, you can use the thousand-year calendar to pull out the ruling elements of any Month or day and use these elements to analyze your own good and bad days. The stem and branch elements of the years for a hundred years are at the end of this book.

When the year elements hurt the SELF-element, that is when using feng shui and incorporating element therapy into the arrangement of homes and offices become truly amazing for nullifying the effect of the year's harmful elements. And when these eight characters findings are used in conjunction with flying star charts the result is even more effective, and truly awesome.

Make a note of the element that symbolizes your wealth element because this indicates the source of your wealth. When your wealth element is present in your chart in quantities that excite you, then check what your wealth element is:

WOOD, the source of your wealth is associated with, plants and anything that grows. This includes plantations, printing, publishing, gardens, landscape businesses and so forth.

FIRE, the source of your wealth is associated with electricity, restaurants, lights, lamps, and anything associated with sunshine and fire energy.

WATER, the source of your wealth is associated with water, such as fishing, shipping, cruises, aqua cultures, bars, beverages, water bottling and so forth.

METAL, the source of your wealth is associated with construction, weapons, buildings, planes, vehicles, trains, machines, computers, construction, and so forth.

EARTH, the source of your wealth is land, property, real estate, mining, farming and so forth. Those whose wealth element is EARTH can also make money from the other element related industries. This is because earth is believed to be inherent in all five elements and lie at the core of material luck. You will discover that many of the world's richest men and women have earth as their wealth element. Why is this?

Because it is really through ownership of property that many people become billionaires − land values keep increasing. In Economics we have a term for this. I am an Economist and I know that property is the basis of the greatest appreciation of wealth because of what we Economists term as the Ricardo's theory of rent. This Theory is based on the premise that land is the one factor that will always get scarcer over time. So if earth is your wealth element, you should endeavour to put as much of your investments as possible into real estate. This will be your greatest source of unearned income, of your wealth. As many of you know. Wealth does not come from

earned incomes. It comes mainly from capital appreciation. Since we are also living though an earth period (Period 8), it favours property appreciation.

SAMPLE CHART READING

To assist you to make a reading of your wealth potential, here is a sample reading. This is the chart of young Patrick whose chart we first saw in the previous chapter. ... let us examine the eight characters as well as the ten year luck pillars to investigate whether there is wealth potential in this young man's chart.

Patrick's Self-element is weak FIRE. So his favourable elements are wood and water. Note his chart is lacking in water.

His WEALTH element is METAL and from the chart we see there are 2 metal in his chart. So there is definitely wealth potential.

His FIRE self although weak (due to the presence of Earth and metal in his chart and also that he is born in the autumn season) nevertheless has two other fire to keep him reasonably strong. There is also wood to produce fire. This suggests that he has enough resources to actualize his wealth potential with little difficulty. The chart shows that his wealth is partly made by him (as indicated by the yang metal in the HOUR pillar) and partly inherited (as indicated by the Rooster

This chart shows hidden wealth luck. Hidden metal is created by the combination of the Dragon and Rooster branches in the YEAR and MONTH pillars.

PAHT CHEE CHART - PATRICK

HOUR HEAVENLY STEM	DAY HEAVENLY STEM	MONTH HEAVENLY STEM	YEAR HEAVENLY STEM
庚 Yang Metal	丙 Yang Fire	丁 Yin Fire	丙 Yang Fire
YANG METAL	YANG FIRE	YIN FIRE	YANG FIRE

HOUR EARTHLY BRANCH	DAY EARTHLY BRANCH	MONTH EARTHLY BRANCH	YEAR EARTHLY BRANCH
寅 Yang Wood	戌 Yang Earth	酉 Yin Metal	辰 Yang Earth
TIGER WOOD	DOG EARTH	ROOSTER METAL	DRAGON EARTH

metal in the MONTH pillar) from his mother or some other matriarchal figure such as a grandmother, an aunty or even a mother in law. And because the element itself is METAL it suggests that his wealth will be made from buildings or construction, or other metal related industry.

HIDDEN ELEMENTS

Patrick's chart also indicates powerful hidden wealth luck in his chart – there is hidden metal created by the combination of rooster and dragon. This hidden metal suggests that Patrick's source of wealth comes from either someone born with a dragon or rooster branch in his/her chart. Hidden wealth elements are potent indicators of wealth.

Take note that any analysis always takes a big picture look at the eight characters chart itself before moving on to the ten-year luck pillars, and this is because it is so important to look at the complete basket of elements. Thus you can see that Patrick's chart lacks water so the appearance of water in the luck pillars is good for Patrick even though superficially water can weaken the self-element. Here therefore we look on water as enhancing wood, which in turn strengthens fire.

Next we now look at Patrick's ten year luck pillars.

Patrick's luck pillars suggest he has some excellent periods when luck is on his side. Remember Patrick's favourable element is WOOD followed by WATER. These elements will strengthen him. He needs

PATRICK'S TEN YEAR LUCK PILLARS

	12-21 years	22-31 years	32-41 years	42-51 years	52-61 years	62-71 years	72-81 years
Good pillar indicated by star		★		★	★		
Heavenly Stems	Yin Earth	Yang Metal	Yin Metal	Yang Water	Yin Water	Yang Wood	Yin Wood
Earthly Branch	Pig Yin Water	Rat Yang Water	Ox Yin Earth	Tiger Yang Wood	Rabbit Yin Wood	Dragon Yang Earth	Snake Yin Fire

these elements in his luck pillars for him to actualize the promise of wealth luck in his chart. Based on this premise we draw the following conclusions:

To start with, note that his excellent years for making money start when he is 22 to 31 years of age when WATER and METAL are present. Here the water balances his basket of elements. Water is a balancing element that strengthens him while the presence of METAL brings the promise of financial success. He still needs WOOD. So he will benefit during years, which also feature the WOOD element.

Between the age of 32 years to 41 years, Patrick also has the potential for making money and accumulating wealth. The presence of the OX earth here suggests that these are years when he will demonstrate great creativity and intelligence to create wealth. This is because Earth, being the element that is produced by the SELF-element, signifies intelligence. The motivating force behind Patrick's determination to make money will be his children. This is because Earth also signifies his children.

But from the chart, big money is likely to materialize during the years when both WOOD and WATER are present. These are the ten years when Patrick is between 42 to 51 years and also between 52 to 61 years. These two years coincide with his two favourable elements of Wood and Water. Because he is a Yang Fire person the compatibility favour the Yang years (between 42 to 51 years) for making money. It favours the Yin years (between 52 to 61 years) for family. If you want to go even deeper into the analysis to pinpoint the exact year and age when Patrick will strike it big we will need to look at the hundred years calendar.

Thus when Patrick is 42 to 51 years of age, since he was born in 1976, these will be the years from 2018 to 2027. If we consult the calendar below and look for the years when the elements are favourable for Patrick we find these are the years 2022 to 2023 which are years when the elements are wood and water. So we can immediately confirm that Patrick's most successful years from a financial viewpoint will be when he is 46 and 47 years old.

12 YEAR CALENDER OF YEARS FROM 2005 INDICATING THE ELEMENTS OF EACH YEAR

Animal	Year	Branch	Stem
ROOSTER	2005	Yin Metal	Yin Wood
DOG	2006	Yang Metal	Yang Fire
BOAR	2007	Yin Water	Yin Fire
RAT	2008	Yang Water	Yang Earth
OX	2009	Yin Earth	Yin Earth
TIGER	2010	Yang Wood	Yang Metal
RABBIT	2011	Yin Wood	Yin Metal
DRAGON	2012	Yang Earth	Yang Water
SNAKE	2013	Yin Fire	Yin Water
HORSE	2014	Yang Fire	Yang Wood
SHEEP	2015	Yin Earth	Yin Wood
MONKEY	2016	Yang Metal	Yang Fire

So what does Patrick's moneymaking prospects like in 2005/2006?

In 2005 the heavenly stem is wood and the earthly branch is metal. This is thus potentially a very good year for Patrick. Wood will strengthen him thereby enabling him to benefit from his wealth luck signified by the presence of metal. 2005 is a Rooster year. Rooster is the secret friend of the Dragon so Patrick being a Dragon year person is certain to benefit from the chi energy of the Rooster in 2005.

In 2006 the elements are fire and earth. Fire signifies friends for Patrick and it also strengthens his self-element, but earth exhausts him so 2006 is not anywhere as favourable as 2005. It is also the year of the Dog who is the natural enemy of the Dragon. So the year 2006 is a year when Patrick needs to be extra careful and watch his back. This is not a year to take risks, indulge in dangerous sport or start any new ventures.

"FOLLOW MY LEADER LUCK"

If you find that your WEALTH luck element is completely missing from your eight characters chart, it suggests that you must activate what is known as a "Follow my leader" kind of luck. This means you must cause your success luck to be reflected to you from someone else, someone who is your mentor, your boss or simply someone you respect in authority over you. This can cause wealth luck to eventually materialize for you.

FOUR GROUPS OF HOROSCOPE ALLIES

RAT	DRAGON	MONKEY	OX	SNAKE	ROOSTER
TIGER	HORSE	DOG	RABBIT	SHEEP	BOAR

This kind of wealth luck comes when there is hidden wealth luck in your chart i.e. when the wealth luck is in the hidden elements of your eight characters and so, is not immediately obvious. The hidden elements are created from the combination of the stems or of the branch elements in the chart. So if your chart shows no signs of wealth luck, it can mean that your wealth luck potential is not immediately obvious. It does not mean you will never become comfortably rich, as it is likely that there are areas in which you excel and become a success. It does. mean that you are unlikely to become seriously wealthy, become another Bill Gates or reach tycoon status.

Remember that in personal luck forecasting success does not always equate with money. Nor does money necessarily go hand in hand with status, power or fame. Each of these aspects of life is a different type of energy. So one can be rich without being famous, skilled without being rich, or powerful and influential without being very clever.

The world if filled with frustrated geniuses and dumb millionaires! Rarely does a single person have it all. As for money luck however, wealth does not necessarily equate with happiness. Hence it is a balanced basket of elements that signify the really good life, not one that is skewed too heavily in only one single aspect of happiness.

ACTIVATING FOLLOW MY LEADER LUCK

The best way to activate follow my leader luck is to associate yourself with people whose self-element is favourable to yours. This could be a little difficult as most people's self-element is not immediately accessible. You need to generate their paht chee chart before you can determine their self-element.

This is where knowing about horoscope allies and secret friends among the Chinese animal signs can be so useful.

HOROSCOPE SECRET FRIENDS

RAT & OX

TIGER & BOAR

RABBIT & DOG

DRAGON & ROOSTER

SNAKE & MONKEY

HORSE & SHEEP

When you find yourself lacking wealth luck it is helpful looking for mentor luck by associating with others who have it and whose animal sign can benefit you due to intrinsic astrological affinity.

All you need then is their year of birth. Usually your boss, or a mentor figure, an uncle or aunt, an elder brother or sister who is successful in his or her field would be a great source of mentor luck for you and if their animal sign based on their YEAR earthly branch has an affinity with yours then working for them or going into partnership with them, and accepting yourself in a junior capacity would be very beneficial indeed. When you are in a 'follow my leader" situation, you must really activate your allies luck. Place images of horoscope allies on your desk and be on the lookout for job situations where you can develop a career with people who are your horoscope allies.

So take note of your allies from the illustration above. There are many beneficial uses in knowing your allies – what the Chinese

refer to as the triangles of affinity. So note the four sets of allies shown on page 77.

In addition to the horoscope allies, there are also combinations of the horoscope between different animal signs, which are even closer and where there is even greater affinity and benefits. These are known as the secret friends of the horoscope and the pairings of these combinations are usually very auspicious. See table above.

To find out your secret friend you will need the YEAR of birth as these pairings are based on the YEAR of birth. When you able to find your secret friend, going into any kind of partnership with such people usually bring beneficial financial gains.

Thus note that when the RAT combines with the OX, there will always be harmony. What results is EARTH and if this is also your WEALTH luck element then the combination will bring financial benefits.

A combination between the TIGER and the BOAR results in WOOD being the element created. If WOOD is your wealth element, your secret friend will bring you financial gains.

friends in the eight characters chart creates a new and hidden element.

The RABBIT and the DOG combining results in the FIRE element and also brings an unexpected windfall. This is quite a terrific combination indeed especially if your wealth element is fire.

The DRAGON and the ROOSTER are divine pals and their combination results in METAL. If this is your WEALTH element, the combination brings prosperity to you.

The SNAKE and the MONKEY creates the WATER element and if this is your WEALTH luck element the combination will bring you a great deal of speculative luck.

Finally the HORSE combines with the SHEEP to produce FIRE element and this brings you the luck of a powerful patron, someone rich and influential who will benefit you both. If FIRE is also your WEALTH luck element there are financial benefits as well.

The combination of the secret friends of the Chinese horoscope is one of the most powerfully beneficial combinations of earthly branches in the eight characters system. If you will recall, we saw earlier that having two animal signs that correspond to secret

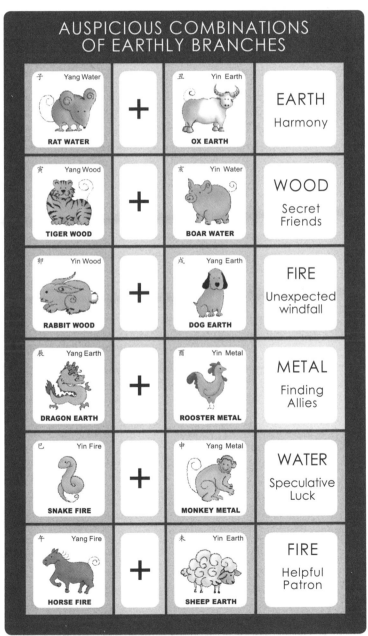

AUSPICIOUS COMBINATIONS OF EARTHLY BRANCHES

子 Yang Water		丑 Yin Earth		
RAT WATER	+	OX EARTH		EARTH Harmony
寅 Yang Wood		亥 Yin Water		
TIGER WOOD	+	BOAR WATER		WOOD Secret Friends
卯 Yin Wood		戌 Yang Earth		
RABBIT WOOD	+	DOG EARTH		FIRE Unexpected windfall
辰 Yang Earth		酉 Yin Metal		
DRAGON EARTH	+	ROOSTER METAL		METAL Finding Allies
巳 Yin Fire		申 Yang Metal		
SNAKE FIRE	+	MONKEY METAL		WATER Speculative Luck
午 Yang Fire		未 Yin Earth		
HORSE FIRE	+	SHEEP EARTH		FIRE Helpful Patron

PARTNERS IN PROSPERITY

You can use the graphic of secret friends illustrated above to help you find a business or life partner who is not only compatible with you but with whom you will have great success luck. Start with your animal horoscope sign based on your YEAR of birth, and then see if the secret friend allied to your animal sign results in a combination that also signifies your WEALTH element. If it is, then you must seek out someone who is your secret friend. Forming a joint venture with this secret friend is sure to bring you financial benefits.

EXAMPLES

Going back to Patricks chart (page 76). Note that Patrick is a fire dragon. His WEALTH element is METAL. So he needs to look for someone whose animal sign is Rooster and then go into partnership with that person. Their partnership will bear financial fruits if it is a business partnership. If the union is one of marriage, their combined luck is certain to bring wealth and also attract many new allies into your life.

Next consider the case of Jessica is an earth Sheep. Her Wealth element is EARTH. Her secret friend is the Horse and while allying with a Horse person is excellent for her it does not result in financial gain. Instead it results in FIRE, which to Jessica signifies intelligence, creativity and aspirations. This suggests that a joint venture or a marriage union with a Horse will inspire Jessica to great heights. Jessica does have wealth potential in her chart. Indeed she has 5 Earth, which could be too much. In her, getting rich means having plenty of Water element nearby to strengthen her SELF.

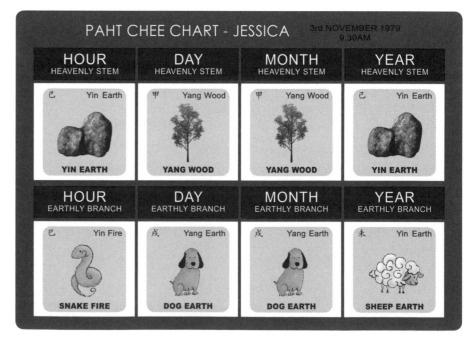

PAHT CHEE CHART - JESSICA   3rd NOVEMBER 1979   9.30AM

HOUR HEAVENLY STEM	DAY HEAVENLY STEM	MONTH HEAVENLY STEM	YEAR HEAVENLY STEM
己 Yin Earth	甲 Yang Wood	甲 Yang Wood	己 Yin Earth
YIN EARTH	YANG WOOD	YANG WOOD	YIN EARTH

HOUR EARTHLY BRANCH	DAY EARTHLY BRANCH	MONTH EARTHLY BRANCH	YEAR EARTHLY BRANCH
巳 Yin Fire	戌 Yang Earth	戌 Yang Earth	未 Yin Earth
SNAKE FIRE	DOG EARTH	DOG EARTH	SHEEP EARTH

Part Four

ANALYSING
THE CHART
FOR TIMING

WHEN WILL MY GOOD YEARS BEGIN?

WHEN WILL I GET MY FIRST REAL BIG BREAK?

12 PHASES OF LIFE

*T*he Chinese content that a person's life begins at the time of Conception and ends at the time of Burial. This is a person's life span and for purposes of personal forecasting our life span is divided into twelve phases. The length of each phase is unequal. The early part of life comprises the first five phases from conception through babyhood, infancy, childhood and adolescence and these last for approximately twenty years.

So it can be said that life really "starts" around the age of 21 years when the life cycle reaches the "Coming of age" phase, which is when a person is deemed to have come to adulthood. This is the age when we will benefit most from any good luck potential that lies inherent in our chart. This is because it is at this age that we have the most amount of sheng chi or growth energy.

So this is the time when we will benefit enormously if our life chart reveals good luck forces (or sheng chi) as indicated in the elements of our charts & luck pillars. Note that the Coming of Age phase is followed by Adulthood, Maturity and Retirement. After that the life cycle goes into decline characterized by ageing, sickness and eventually, death.

The Chinese focus on the 30 to 40 years of our life that fall between the Coming of Age phase and the Retirement phase. These are our active years. Good fortune sheng chi and favourable element years (as indicated in the charts) are best, when they occur during these active years. So when you look at your luck pillars focus in on these years. When good luck comes too early we are too young to make the most of it and when luck comes too late we might be too old and too unhealthy to enjoy the good fortune. It is also considered to be a better life chart when the later years look better than the early years. When you are still a child no matter how hard your life is, you will feel it less than when you are older. The important years to focus in are thus the "active" years of your life span.

For instance wealth or career luck is of little use if it occurs in the chart during the age of decline. When we are old how are we able to fully benefit from any kind of luck. If wealth luck shows up too early in your chart, it is also of little use since it will not mean you are wealthy, but only indicate that your growing up years were spent amidst wealthy surroundings. You could have lived in a mansion but you could have been the child of the housekeeper and not the child of the owner. In any case wealth luck at too early an age is considered premature.

The same is true for relationships and family luck. It is best that indications of marriage and children luck should show up during the coming of age period of one's life. When it comes too late in life it suggests that one misses out on some crucial years.

So for luck predictions and personal forecasts to be meaningful, the issue of timing is important.

To answer the question, "when will my luck begin" the answer is, "Your luck should begin when you come of age at around 21 years old."

More to the point is "what kind of good luck will come my way as soon as I come of age i.e. as soon as I am in a position to benefit from it." This is the crucial question.

FIVE FORCES OF CHI

Actually there are five important kinds of chi energy that we are all born with. These five forces of chi can be roughly translated as FATE chi, FAMILY chi, MENTOR chi, PROSPERITY chi & OPPORTUNITY chi. This set of chi energy are different from the five types of luck dealt with in the earlier chapters. These five types of chi energy are what everyone is born with. So everyone has these five types of chi energy in their charts.

The difference between everyone is that each of these different types of chi occur at different times for different people. Some people start life with Prosperity chi, others with Family Chi and so forth. It is this which determines the timing of one's success in life.

More, each person at best benefits from only three types of Chi during the period between the Coming of age years and Retirement years. So in everyone's life there will always be two kinds of Chi which kick in either too early (during childhood) or too late (during the declining years). This means that we will really benefit from three out of the five types of Chi luck.

To identify the kind of Chi that enters into your life chart during the Coming of age phase you need to get familiar with the five types of Chi luck, and determine what element represents your FATE Chi. The five types of Chi are represented by the five elements

First, you need to determine your FATE ELEMENT. FATE is the premier Chi. It determines the element of the other Chi luck forces. So note that the FATE element is the element of the Earthly branch of your YEAR of birth (which is also the element of your animal horoscope). So you see, the animal sign we are born with is very revealing.

TABLE SHOWING THE FIVE TYPES OF CHI

If your FATE chi is... →	WOOD	FIRE	EARTH	METAL	WATER
Your Family Chi is	FIRE	EARTH	METAL	WATER	WOOD
Your Mentor Chi is	EARTH	METAL	WATER	WOOD	FIRE
Prosperity Chi is	METAL	WATER	WOOD	FIRE	EARTH
Opportunity Chi is	WATER	WOOD	FIRE	EARTH	METAL

Once you know your FATE chi ELEMENT you can determine the corresponding elements of the four remaining types of Chi by using the table above.

You need to determine when each of the five types of Chi makes its appearance in your life. This will indicate when each type of Chi brings helpful sheng chi or growth energy to strengthen and assist you. Determining this requires two additional pieces of information from your eight characters chart ie,

a. The element of the Earthly Branch of your MONTH pillar

b. The element of the Heavenly Stem of your YEAR pillar.

These two elements will combine to reveal your Coming of age element . Once you know this coming of age element, you can use it to determine the kind of Chi that will be at its zenith when you are at the Coming of Age phase of your life i.e. when you are in your twenties. You will need your FATE element as well to determine this.

HOUR PILLAR	DAY PILLAR	MONTH PILLAR	YEAR PILLAR
Heavenly Stem	Heavenly Stem	Heavenly Stem	(b) Heavenly Stem
Earthly branch	Earthly Branch	Earthly Branch (a)	Earthly Branch

EXAMPLE:

Patrick is a fire dragon. His chart is reproduced below for easy reference.

Patrick's FATE element is EARTH, which is the element of the dragon (the earthly branch of the YEAR of birth).

Next we need to know Patrick's Coming of age element. For this we need to determine the Earthly branch of the MONTH pillar (which is Rooster yin metal as shown in his chart reproduced here), and the Heavenly stem of the Year pillar. (which is Yang Fire)

HOUR PILLAR	DAY PILLAR	MONTH PILLAR	YEAR PILLAR
HEAVENLY STEM	HEAVENLY STEM	HEAVENLY STEM	HEAVENLY STEM
Yang Metal	Yang Fire	Yin Fire	Yang Fire
EARTHLY BRANCH	EARTHLY BRANCH	EARTHLY BRANCH	EARTHLY BRANCH
Tiger Wood	Dog Earth	Rooster Metal	Dragon Earth

EARTHLY BRANCH \ HEAVENLY STEM	YANG WOOD	YIN WOOD	YANG FIRE	YIN FIRE	YANG EARTH	YIN EARTH
YANG WATER	Water*	Wood	Wood*	Fire	Earth	Earth
YIN EARTH	Water	Wood	Wood*	Fire	Fire*	Earth
YANG WOOD	Water	Wood	Wood	Wood*	Fire	Earth
YIN WOOD	Water	Wood	Wood	Wood	Fire	Earth
YANG EARTH	Water	Wood*	Wood*	Wood	Fire	Earth
YIN FIRE	Water	Wood	Wood	Wood	Fire	Earth
YANG FIRE	Metal*	Water	Water	Wood	Wood	Fire
YIN EARTH	Metal	Water	Water	Wood	Wood	Fire
YANG METAL	Metal	Water	Water	Wood	Wood	Fire
YIN METAL	Metal	Water	**Water**	Water*	Wood	Wood*
YANG EARTH	Metal	Metal	Water	Water	Wood	Wood
YIN WATER	Metal	Metal	Water	Water	Wood	Wood

YANG METAL	YIN METAL	YANG WATER	YIN WATER
Earth	Metal	Water*	Water
Earth	Metal	Metal	Fire
Earth	Metal	Metal	Water
Earth	Earth*	Metal	Water
Earth	Earth*	Metal	Water
Earth	Earth*	Metal	Water
Fire*	Earth	Metal	Metal
Fire	Earth	Earth*	Metal
Fire	Earth	Earth	Water
Fire	Earth	Earth	Earth*
Fire	Fire*	Earth	Earth
Fire	Fire	Earth	Earth

Next referring to the Table here, we look to see what element is created by combining the yang fire of the Year Pillar with the yin metal branch of the Month Pillar.

You can see that Patrick's coming of age element is WATER (marked in bold in red in the Table here).

In the table here take note of the elements with an *. Thus
- Water* means the coming of age element can be water or wood
- Wood* means the coming of age element can be wood or fire
- Fire* means the coming of age element can be fire or earth
- Earth* means the coming of age element can be earth or metal
- Metal* means the coming of age element can be metal or water.

Note that when the Coming of age has two elements both types of Chi luck resulting from the combination exerts their influence.

EXAMPLE:

In our example Patrick's FATE element is EARTH, and his Coming of Age element is WATER. So using the Table of Chi luck we can see that in Patrick's case his MENTOR CHI force will be at its zenith during his coming of age. This is because for Patrick his mentor luck is represented by WATER.

> **What this suggests is that Patrick benefits from the help of someone influential and important who will act as a mentor during crucial times. It is not necessarily his father nor is it necessary that the mentor is a man. It can be an aunty or a mother in law – whoever it is, this person or persons (yes there can be more than one), will be someone who will give him the means to get started in life. The mentor luck will give Patrick a strong helping hand to jump-start his professional life.**

Occurring at this stage of life is most beneficial to Patrick and mentor luck at this stage usually suggests financial aid to further one's study OR a job opportunity that opens many possibilities. Once you have locked in the Chi luck, which starts your life, you can then identify the element that signify the other two types of Chi luck that will be at its zenith during your adulthood and maturity years.

In the case of Patrick, his MENTOR luck Chi is followed by PROSPERITY Chi luck (WOOD), and then by OPPORTUNITY Chi luck (FIRE).

You can say then that Patrick benefits from his MENTOR luck and from his PROSPERITY luck forces. The Opportunity luck coming late in maturity will not be of much benefit since by then Patrick is already nearing retirement and will probably not have the energy to make fullest use of OPPORTUNITY coming his way.

Once Patrick has identified the element that represents the important Chi luck forces in his life, he can look out for these elements in his ten-year luck pillars. In this case we are looking for WATER (which represents his mentor luck) and WOOD, which represents his wealth luck. If we find these elements also make an appearance in his luck pillars then the sheng chi representing these forces will strengthen considerably. If we do not find them, then they will be lacking in their influence as the chi energy in that case is weak.

FINDING YOUR CHI LUCK

*T*est your own CHI luck before proceeding further. See if you can put together the few pieces of information referred to from your own eight characters chart, and identify the elements that signify your different types of CHI luck.

Next see which type of CHI dominates your chart during your Coming of Age phase.

Note that the Coming of Age element reveals the kind of head start you will get at the point of time you are going out into the world. This is simply such an important time of anyone's life that any life prediction should really start from here.

For instance, if you are lucky enough to start out with PROSPERITY luck (probably rich parents or a rich benefactor) or if you start out with OPPORTUNITY luck (such as getting an excellent job offer), then you will already have a head start over others.

It is up to you to make the best of any initial good fortune that comes your way. Everyone starts with at least some weighting of one the five types of luck. The difference amongst people is how much weight each one has because in reality ALL of the five forces of luck bring good fortune.

Some people fritter away their good resources at the start of life. Others work at enhancing their good fortune. This aspect – your own actions, attitudes and ethics - will be what determines the results of one's initial good fortune. Destiny only shows your heaven luck, and offer clues on how to improve material earth luck, but it is your one's decisions and how well and smart one works that makes up the mankind luck that will transform good fortune into magnificent success as one grows into maturity. On the other hand, one could simply waste it all away. It is up to the individual.

If your Coming of age element corresponds to the element of FAMILY luck it means your family is supportive of you. It can also indicate that you start life with a happy marriage and enter into a nesting period when you will be bringing up a family. Many experts also suggest that this kind of luck is excellent when it appears at around one's Retirement or declining years since it suggests good health and a happy family life in one's declining years. It is during these years that this kind of luck is most auspicious.

Meanwhile if you start out with FATE luck, it usually indicates a turning point of some kind. This generally manifests as a momentous and happy occasion or it could also occur as a major tragedy. Fate luck force almost always manifests as some kind of traumatic moment of your life, a time when an important decision is either made by you or is forced upon you. So if it occurs at the start of life it is probably a lot more meaningful since it is then that we have the energy and resilience to benefit from any traumatic or life-changing event.

When the coming of age chi force is MENTOR luck this indicates a helpful person opening doors to opportunity, power and influence for you. It is patronage at its best. It is an exceptionally good luck force to have either at the start of one's adult life or during the years that correspond to one's adult and mature years.

So once you know the luck force that corresponds with your Coming of Age, you can identify when other types of luck will occur. This is based on the natural cycle of elements. Thus FATE luck is followed by FAMILY, which in turn is followed by MENTOR, then PROSPERITY and then OPPORTUNITY.

When your luck force at the Coming of Age is MENTOR CHI then in the next Phase of life, which will be adulthood, you will enjoy WEALTH CHI, and in your maturity years you will enjoy OPPORTUNITY CHI. Generally the other two types of CHI are regarded as inaccessible to your current life since they will occur during the Childhood phase or during your declining years. Always follow the sequence, which is repeated below:

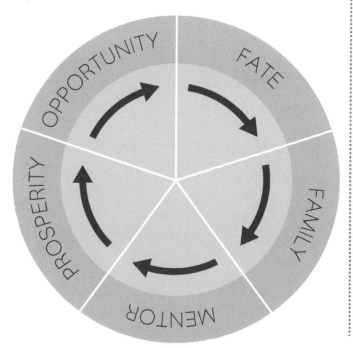

Please note that the mere occurrence and timing of the five types of CHI luck in your paht chee chart does not guarantee that you will automatically become rich during a PROSPERITY CHI phase or GET MARRIED during FAMILY CHI phase.

The manifestation of the CHI luck indicated depends equally on their appearance in your ten-year luck pillars, and when they ripen, the effects can be positive or negative.

It is positive when the element that corresponds to the CHI LUCK indicated has a strong weighting in your chart (i.e. at least 2 or 3) but not more and definitely not less. So for instance if EARTH indicates PROSPERITY luck for you, and you have 3 or 4 Earth elements in your paht chee chart, and the PROSPERITY luck force enters your chart during the Adulthood phase of your life then it is very likely that you will become very rich. Why? Because all the elements are working in your favour !

HOW FIVE TYPES OF CHI MANIFEST FOR YOU

*t*he five types of chi luck are listed as FATE, FAMILY, MENTOR, PROSPERITY and OPPORTUNITY LUCK. We have seen that how these luck forces manifest in a person's life depends as much on the timing of its appearance as on the number of times its equivalent element appears in the eight characters chart. This is referred to as weighting in the chart.

These two pieces of information indicate the strength, magnitude and nature of the LUCK. When the weighting of the element in question is zero you can ignore it altogether. And if you discover that METAL is the element that stands for prosperity luck and there is no sign of any metal in your chart, you can rightly conclude you do not have the destiny to become very prosperous.

This does not mean you will be poor, it merely means you will not come into a windfall or be able to accumulate assets. You will probably have other types of luck. Sometimes there may be other signs of wealth luck on your chart that are related to your SELF element (covered in the preceding chapters)

Likewise if your FAMILY luck element is WOOD (or any of the other elements) and this element is completely missing from your chart, it suggests that you are sorely lacking in marriage and family luck. Chances are you could become a confirmed bachelor or spinster. You will have to look then for other indications of marriage and family related luck related to your SELF-element. OR you can activate peach blossom luck based on your earthly branch (animal sign) of your YEAR pillar.

PEACH BLOSSOM LUCK

Anyone can use this method to activate or speed up their marriage luck. It is particularly effective when done during a year when the astrological forces indicate that peach blossom luck is strong. (e.g. the year 2005 is a year when peach blossom luck is very strong). This happens in cycles of nine years, so after 2005, the next year when it will be strong again will be the year 2014. However activating peach blossom luck can be done anytime and it always brings excellent FAMILY Chi, which implies marriage luck for those who are single.

if you lack family luck, and find it hard to get married or find someone special, then activating your peach blossom luck creates strong marriage luck for you. Here's how to activate peach blossom luck.

if you are born in an Ox, Snake or Rooster year placing a HORSE in the South of your sleeping space will bring peach blossom luck.

if you are a Rat, Dragon or Monkey, placing a golden Rooster in the West of your sleeping space is excellent.

if you are a Rabbit, Sheep or Boar, placing a blue Rat in the North of your sleeping space is excellent.

if you are a Tiger, Horse or Dog, placing a green Rabbit in the East of your sleeping space is excellent.

HOW EACH TYPE OF LUCK MATERIALIZES

FATE LUCK is probably the most dramatic of the five chi luck forces. Usually it suggests a particular moment in your life, which signifies a major turning point. This can mean anything from an unexpected inheritance, a stroke of fortune, a tragedy, a death in the family, a marriage, the entrée of a special new person into your life, a new job, a change of country, a transformation of lifestyle – anything at all that suggests a VERY major change in your life a turning point.

The magnitude of the change and the nature of the change are affected by the weighting of the element that corresponds to the FATE element.

- Usually when the FATE element is WOOD it refers to something in the creative field such as painting, dancing, or any kind of performing arts. Some experts equate WOOD with industry areas that are based on plants such as paper, furniture or plantation businesses. This is certainly a plausible interpretation. Wood also suggests a growth spurt or a stunting of growth. This means any event or incident that causes you to grow up fast. Teenage children who lose their parents for instance are forced to grow up overnight as they come to terms with tragedy. So losing a parent or being forced to live in another country or parents separating – these and other similar dramatic events are the kind of traumatic events suggested by FATE luck chi represented by Wood.

- If the FATE element is FIRE it suggests a change of direction in one's career, perhaps a transfer, a new job or being made an amazing offer. The offer could well be related to industry areas that signify FIRE element such as bright lights, restaurant business, working in hot countries – interpretation can be as creative as you wish but imagination should never get out of control. FIRE chi can also suggest tragedy or accident associated with fire.

- If your FATE element is EARTH it usually means the successful and perhaps unexpected acquisition of land. A turning point could take place, which has its source in anything to do with property. The vastness of interpretation possibilities is what makes it so much easier to make predictions after the event! When you are attempting a life reading let your mind stay open to signals coming to you from your inner consciousness. All of us are closet psychics and we should never ignore messages that emanate from our inner minds. Whenever you read your eight characters chart, do not ignore your inner mind which usually gets activated to help you interpret the charts. This also comes with experience and practice so that the more charts you read the more adept you become at it.

- If your FATE element is METAL it means a sudden fortune, a windfall of sorts that result in increased income levels. Usually this element is associated with the creation of wealth, and here do note that wealth is a little different from income. Wealth means assets, and is often associated with a windfall. It also suggests a commercial business or project, rather than a career. So this can mean an unexpected inheritance, winning the lottery, getting a fat profitable contract or the sudden success of something you invested in earlier.

- And if your FATE element is WATER it always means a journey of some kind, a change of direction that involves travel. WATER also means communication or enhanced income levels. Anything that suggests a flow is associated with this element so a transformation that brings an enhanced flow of income could well be indicated by the WATER element. The journey can have negative or positive connotations so how the journey turns out – whether for good or bad again depends on the way you react to the journey. It also depends on how the lement reacts to and combines with other elements in the chart

FAMILY LUCK generally indicates a nesting period. When it occurs at the start of adulthood it can be predicting a forthcoming happy love affair or marriage, which brings benefits and fulfillment. When this LUCK force comes at the end of a life span, it suggests a happy retirement where good health and happiness prevails. Family luck always indicates a sense of contentment, a feeling of satisfaction and great happiness. Once again the magnitude of its manifestation is directly related to the weighting of the element that corresponds to it in the chart. For judging the weighting you can use the basket of eight elements or the basket of twelve elements. (ie. if there are hidden elements)

When family luck occurs during childhood it means your family looked after you well. If it occurs in your declining years it can mean that you are well looked after during your old age. But generally FAMILY luck Chi occurring during Childhood or Old age can also suggest a lack of family (little probability of getting married or having children). Another way to interpret this is that if the element that signifies FAMILY luck Chi is missing from the eight characters chart and also missing from the ten-year luck pillars, then this is a strong indication that marriage and family luck are lacking. A woman having this in her chart will find it hard to get married.

- If FAMILY LUCK is WOOD, it indicates pleasurable pursuits of family life. Wood also suggests growth and here it means growth in the family's fortunes as well as growth in the size of the family. The WOOD element as Family luck always suggests good descendants and especially good sons who will bring honour to the family. If you are the Patriarch of a family, getting Family luck In your RETIREMENT years and if it is WOOD element, it means you will live long enough to see your children and grandchildren bringing honour to the family name. You will participate in their success as much as they participate in your good name, and your good health.

- If your FAMILY LUCK element is FIRE it means the family becomes better off due to career success. FIRE always suggests attainment of heights of recognition and fame so that when

it indicates your FAMILY it suggests a family project or business enjoying a spurt of success. It also suggests that the family gains recognition and success as an entity. There is good name and honourable recognition. People will look up to you.

- If the FAMILY LUCK element is EARTH it suggests meditative and spiritual pursuits. Here EARTH suggests a period of being grounded when thoughts turn to fundamental things of life. Sometimes it means the rise of spirituality and spiritual pursuits. It could indicate a time of retreat when you go within yourself in search of spiritual truths. I have seen this feature in people who take time off from pursuing material success by entering into a period of retreat. It is interesting since FAMILY LUCK would suggest enhanced bonding with family, yet sometimes it can mean a "tuning inwards" if the indicative element is FIRE.

- If the FAMILY LUCK element is METAL, it indicates the family's possessions will increase and lifestyle will take a quantum leap. This is the element that suggests wealth and asset enhancement. It can also mean finding a new project or business which benefits the entire family, bringing all the members closer together.

- If the FAMILY LUCK element is WATER, it means the family will gain in prestige as a result of you being honoured. This is a particularly good reading when the FAMILY LUCK occurs towards the ending phase of one's life because then it tends to suggest reaping the benefits of a life well lived. Water also means being well off materially and financially.

Signs of romance, love and marriage in your eight characters chart are indicated by the presence of the element that represents FAMILY in your chart. So the first step to finding out if you have the destiny to get married is to first identify whether the element that signifies FAMILY luck is present in your chart. If it is not present in the paht chee then it should at least make an appearance in your luck pillars.

*M*ENTOR LUCK usually refers to the entrée of a powerful and influential patron in your life. It can also refer to getting assistance from a public official, or you catching the eye of a powerful man or woman. It usually manifests in the form of an elevation in status or a major promotion. If it appears during the Coming of age phase of life it is a surefire indicator of a very successful start to your career. A powerful mentor helps you to gain recognition and acceptance. It is a good indication.

If it appears during one's childhood phase it suggests the possession of natural talent or skill. If it makes its appearance during the end of life then it suggests that you will obtain public recognition for all your work and attainments. How long this luck lasts depends on the weighting of this element in your basket of elements, and how beneficial it will be depends on other indications on your eight characters and ten year luck periods.

Mentor luck is almost always accompanied by a rise in one's social status. Often it can mean being conferred an honorary and prestigious title such as a knighthood. Other times it can also mean you are successful in obtaining a high political or corporate position, which you have been eyeing. Mentor luck is especially beneficial when it appears in your chart during the early years of adulthood.

- If MENTOR LUCK it is WOOD it suggests gaining recognition for creative pursuits. The element of WOOD also suggests elevation in status in the performing arts and when it comes to you as MENTOR luck your rise will be fast and phenomenal, catching the attention of peers and competitors alike. You will be able to leap frog over many others less fortunate than you, and you will gain the support of those whose opinion and judgments are important. How long this period lasts depends on the weighting of the element.

- If your MENTOR LUCK is FIRE it suggests that you will gain recognition for your community and charity work – no matter how small or insignificant your contribution it will attract the goodwill of important people thereby propelling you into a different status. If this is a situation that describes you, it will be extremely beneficial if you were to begin associating yourself with charitable institutions, as this will be your entrée to great good fortune indeed.

- If your MENTOR LUCK is EARTH, it indicates that you will receive an award or a special prestigious assignment. Sometimes when particularly strong in the charts, it can mean gaining an Ambassadorship, or a Governorship so what is suggested is a very high position, similar to the Mandarins of the Chinese Court gaining high status. The appointment may be unexpected but as long as you are within a good period of your life and the weighting of EARTH in your basket of elements is strong, you will enjoy all the perks of attaining high office. If this luck force

comes to you towards the end of your life, you could miss out on enjoying your rise in status.

- If MENTOR LUCK is METAL, it indicates financial support for your entire worthy causes. And if it is WATER it suggests the attainment of great literary success and recognition.

PROSPERITY LUCK as the name implies refers to riches and wealth. If it makes an appearance at the Coming of age phase of your life and its associated element has a high weighting, these are very strong indications that you will become rich. If the weighting of the wealth element is 3 out of 8; it is a strong indication of great wealth.

The prosperity luck read as part of the five chi luck forces complements the WEALTH luck indicated in the Five aspects of life luck using the relationship of the elements. When both indicators of wealth show the presence of wealth luck in the chart and occurs during the time of active years, then the likelihood of becoming rich is very high indeed.

Usually the exact year when the wealth is made or starts to be made will be during a calendar year, which also has a similar corresponding wealth element or a resource element. So if wealth luck is of interest to you, go slowly and investigate this in your chart. Be careful not to make mistakes in your reading... we don't want you celebrating and finding you made a mistake. Neither do I want you feeling deflated because you mistakenly thought you have no wealth luck!

But if Wealth luck appears at the phase of life that corresponds to the Conception or Childhood stage it means you are born into wealth. This situation may or may not last through your whole life. It depends on many different factors and not all of these factors are related to the destiny charts.

If **WEALTH LUCK** appears at the time of Burial, you could end your life with a great deal of wealth but it will not be you who will enjoy it. It will instead be your descendants who will benefit from the wealth. Thus timing of the occurrence of the WEALTH luck force is of the utmost importance, many experts in Chinese fortune telling interpret the presence of WEALTH luck during the Coming of age phase of life to be the most superior of indications. Wealth luck usually suggests material rewards.

- If WEALTH is represented by the WOOD element, then one's wealth will come from the performing or creative arts. It can thus come from writing, from singing or from dancing. This does not necessarily mean that you are a performer. It is more than likely that you are the producer or financier.

- If WEALTH luck is FIRE then wealth comes from the corporate world or from one's own entrepreneurial skills. FIRE always suggests business and things commercial, for the energy of fire is soaring and upward. Thus it can represent wealth from electricity businesses, or electricity related businesses. But fire can also burn itself out so it needs continuous replenishment. When your WEALTH luck is represented by FIRE, it is a good idea to keep your surrounding space well lit, and ensure that your office and home are bathed with powerful sunshine energy.

- If the WEALTH element is EARTH the source of wealth is land, real estate ventures or construction. Many successful property developers, especially those who have speculated on land have made enormous fortunes when their WEALTH element is land and when this is strongly weighted in their basket of elements. This is indeed one of the strongest indications of wealth arising from asset appreciation.

- If the element is METAL prosperity comes from trading and commerce or from the mining of minerals and metals from the ground. METAL can also wealth made from the stock market through capital appreciation and speculation. METAL element is a hard element but it can be made into liquid energy so METAL is often regarded as the "father of money" since water is often associated with money. Sometimes METAL also indicates petroleum and gas, treasures from the earth.

- And if the WEALTH element is WATER then wealth here suggests a flow of money generated from many different sources. There are those who associate water with the communications businesses such as television, newspaper companies, computers and so forth.

Generally the strongest indication of getting wealthy is when either EARTH or METAL is the element of wealth in your chart.

OPPORTUNITY LUCK is the kind of luck, which brings an opportunity of a lifetime. Unlike FATE luck, it will force you into making a decision. It is best when it appears during the Coming of age phase of life. If it appears early in life, i.e. during childhood for instance, opportunity probably comes from one's family background. This can be manifested as inheriting the job of running the family business or the continuation of a political dynasty. How beneficial this will be for your luck depends on its weighting and the nature of the element that corresponds to it.

In many respects OPPORTUNITY luck is a matter of timing. It suggests that you have the luck to strike at the right moment. From this viewpoint it is an extremely powerful force for beneficial outcomes.

- If the element of OPPORTUNITY is WOOD it indicates that when you have good ideas you must pursue them. Your ideas have the luck and energy to grow and take root, leading you to many other opportunities. So generate confidence!

- If it is FIRE it suggest you must not hesitate in changing career. Fire always suggests a transformation in this situation and when it is representative of your OPPORTUNITY LUCK then during the phase of your life when the chance comes you must not be afraid of accepting change and going for it. Be brave!

- If the element is EARTH, it indicates that a chance will come that requires you to change location and that deciding in favour of the change in location is good. This is similar to the FIRE element except that your chance of a lifetime might require you to relocate to another country. If this is the case you can do so without hesitation. If the chance comes during a time of your life span when it is benefiting from OPPORTUNITY LUCK, and your weighting of the element is strong, the chance will open the door to great success. Be adventurous.

• If the OPPORTUNTY luck element is METAL, it indicates that all your investments during the time when this luck appears in your chart will bring you profits. Your investments will also open new opportunities for you, in that you could meet new people and be confronted with projects that have good potential for success. Be on the lookout for investments.

• If the OPPORTUNITY luck element is WATER it suggests that a chance to travel or change domicile will open fantastic new opportunities. Such opportunities may be to pursue further studies, take on a new appointment or start out a new venture. If you are going through this luck phase you would be advised to grab any of the opportunities indicated. Be discerning.

By now the reader can appreciate how easily one can get confused by the constant references to the five elements and their relationships and it is for this reason that I prefer to always refer to the elements directly rather than in code using the Chinese names for each of the heavenly stems and earthly branches. I prefer to refer to the stems of the four Pillars directly as elements (with a yin or a yang prefix) and to the earthly branches as animal signs. This reduces confusion without taking away any of the essence of paht chee forecasting methods.

ANALYSING THE CHART FOR RELATIONSHIPS

We know by now that the five elements reveal a great mass of information. In addition to what we have covered thus far there is also the question of relationships.

The eight characters chart also reveal a great deal about the influence of parents, siblings, spouses and children. This is because in every chart each of these loved ones in our lives can be identified based on the element relationships as well as the elements that occur on the Pillars themselves.

IS THERE A DIFFERENCE IF THE CHART BELONGS TO A MAN OR WOMAN?

The readings vary according to whether the chart belongs to a man or a woman., especially when the reading pertains to marriage, infidelity and divorce.

FOR MEN

The best way to depict the different people in this man's life is to use a typical sample chart. Shown here:

- Self element is YANG WOOD (Day stem)
- Wife is EARTH conquered by WOOD
- Father is also EARTH conquered by WOOD
- Mother is WATER produces WOOD
- Children is METAL which destroys WOOD
- Siblings is WOOD same as self

In the chart, the HOUSE OF SPOUSE is the DAY branch which in this case is HORSE (Yang fire). Parents are indicated by the MONTH Pillar while Grandparents are indicated by the YEAR pillar.

A MAN'S FOUR PILLARS CHART

HOUR	DAY	MONTH	YEAR
乙 YIN WOOD	甲 YANG WOOD	辛 YIN METAL	丙 YANG FIRE
癸亥	丙午	乙卯	庚申
YIN WATER PIG	YANG FIRE HORSE	YIN WOOD RABBIT	YANG METAL MONKEY

28-3-1956 22:47

FOR WOMEN

When reading a woman's chart all the element relationships are the same except for the following:

- When the self element is yang wood, the husband is METAL which is the element that destroys the self element of Wood.
- The offspring are FIRE which is the element that exhausts the self element of Wood.

Part Five

SPECIAL STARS
IN THE CHART

SPECIAL STARS IN THE CHART

*T*here are special stars whose presence in the eight characters chart can be lucky or unlucky according to the specific attributes of a person's life forecasts. These special stars usually give clues to a person's character and personality, ie. the way the person reacts to adversity and aggravations. They also reveal some special attribute, which the person will have that can be the competitive edge the person possesses through life. These stars are therefore excellent additional indications in personal forecasting of the *eight characters* chart.

1 THE STAR OF THE NOBLEMAN

When this star shows itself in your eight characters chart it suggests that you have the aura of a nobleman which according to legend signifies there will always be someone or something that comes to your aid whenever you need help. This is said to be the luckiest indication to have in one's chart as it means that there will always be helpful people to lend you a hand when you need it. All through your life, at every turning point there will always appear helpful people to assist you resolve predicaments or unblock obstacles. The Chinese name for this star is *Tian Yi Gui Ren* which means *helpful lord from heaven provides assistance.*

Having this star in your chart also indicates

that you are a very intelligent and creative person. You have the amazing skill of transforming adversity and bad luck into life enhancing opportunities. In short you act and react like a true nobleman, strong in the face of adversity and wise during good times. You will have many followers and disciples and this suggests a person who is blessed with this indicated star is generally liked and well respected in his/her community. You will find it easy to get support and encouragement. It is a very auspicious indication in the chart indeed and when the element that indicates the presence of this star is also a favourable element for your chart, the good effects are magnified. Intensity of good fortune always depends on weighting of elements.

Not everyone has the star of the nobleman in their *eight characters* chart. To determine if you have the star of the nobleman look at the **heavenly stem in your DAY pillar** (which is also your Self element) and the **earthly branches in your YEAR pillar**. The following combinations of the STEM and BRANCH in the two Pillars indicate the presence of the Nobleman star in your Year pillar.

The Nobleman star can appear in the chart of a person as well as during specific years. For instance if you have Yang Wood as the heavenly stem in the DAY Pillar of your eight characters chart as well as an OX or a SHEEP in your YEAR pillar you possess the attributes of the Nobleman and during the

LOOKING FOR THE STAR OF THE NOBLEMAN

IF HEAVENLY STEM IN DAY PILLAR IS...	AND EARTHLY BRANCH IN YEAR PILLAR IS...	NOBLEMAN STAR APPEARS IN YEARS OF THE
YANG WOOD	OX or SHEEP	OX or SHEEP
YIN WOOD	RAT or MONKEY	RAT or MONKEY
YANG FIRE	PIG or ROOSTER	PIG or ROOSTER
YIN FIRE	PIG ROOSTER	PIG ROOSTER
YANG EARTH	OX or SHEEP	OX or SHEEP
YIN EARTH	RAT or MONKEY	RAT or MONKEY
YANG METAL	OX or SHEEP	OX or SHEEP
YIN METAL	HORSE or TIGER	HORSE or TIGER
YANG WATER	SNAKE or RABBIT	SNAKE or RABBIT
YIN WATER	SNAKE or RABBIT	SNAKE or RABBIT

years of the OX and SHEEP your success will be like that of a nobleman during that year. If you only have Yang Wood in the Day pillar and you are not going through the years of the OX or the Sheep you will still enjoy the attributes of the Nobleman star in these years.

THREE OTHER NOBLEMEN
In addition to this particular indication of the **Nobleman star**, the eight characters chart can also reveal the additional good fortune of being blessed by one of the three noblemen who are described as coming from heaven, earth and mankind. Each of these three extraordinary gentlemen brings incredible talents and good fortune. When any one of these three noblemen appear in your chart it suggests you are a person of high intelligence, gifted, knowledgeable, classy, learned and most generous. You will be sure to rise to great heights of attainments in your lifetime and no adverse experiences will mar your life. The presence of any one of the three noblemen is indicated by the presence of three arrangements of heavenly

ARRANGEMENT OF STEMS TO INDICATE "NOBLEMEN"

NOBLEMAN	HOUR PILLAR	Heavenly stem DAY PILLAR	Heavenly stem MONTH PILLAR	Heavenly stem YEAR PILLAR
From Heaven	NA	Yang Wood	Yang Earth	Yang Metal
From Earth	NA	Yin Wood	Yang Fire	Yin Fire
From Mankind	NA	Yang Water	Yin Water	Yin Metal

stems in the DAY, MONTH AND YEAR pillars as indicated above. It is imperative that the **heavenly stems** appear exactly in the sequences shown.

Only then would these auspicious stars be deemed to be present in the chart. Of the three the most powerful in its influences bringing attainment luck of the highest scope is the **nobleman from heaven**. He brings power and influence. The nobleman from earth however brings material luck such as wealth and prosperity, fame and fortune, while the nobleman from mankind bring talents and skills. It is not possible to say which of the gifts and assets are better as this depends on how you make the fullest use of the good fortune sent to you.

2 THE STAR OF SCHOLASTIC BRILLIANCE

This presence of the star of scholastic brilliance in the eight c*haracters* chart suggest a person who has a thirst for, and affinity with the pursuit of knowledge. Such people will easily gain great **recognition in the academic fields** of research and teaching as they tend to be hardworking and very smart.

This person will also have the luck to gain honours and academic prizes awarded by international bodies. There is the promise of many different accolades and achievements. As a result this person will attain heights of recognition by peers and colleagues. Those with the presence of this star in their charts are sure to do well in their studies and also stand the chance of gaining scholarships and eminent recognition. In their fields they are highly respected.

This star also indicates a refined person who does not appreciate boorish behavior. He/she is gentle and gracious. However do take note that when taken to extremes a person with too much of the influence of this star (ie when there is more than two such stars in the chart) will tend towards conceit and academic arrogance. This might cause problems in relationships.

Not everyone has the star of the scholastic brilliance in their *eight characters* chart. To determine if you have this academic star look at the **heavenly stem in your DAY pillar** (which is also your SELF element) and search for the required **earthly branch** in any of the four pillars. If the required combination of heavenly stem and earthly branch are present in the combinations shown in the table below you possess the star of scholastic brilliance.

Note that you can have as many as four stars of scholastic brilliance and this is because there are 4 pillars. This will mean that your earthly branches will be the same animal sign and your self element is as indicated. E.g. If your self element is Yang earth, then each Monkey in the earthly branch of each pillar will create a star of scholastic brilliance. Please further note that scholastic brilliance here pertains to examination results and not necessarily indicate a genius intellect. There is an element of recognition indicated by the scholastic start. To benefit from this star all you need is a single star present in the chart. When you have too many scholastic brilliance stars it indicates an obsessive passion for scholarship in a very unbalanced way. It is not considered to be auspicious then.

ARRANGEMENT OF ELEMENTS TO INDICATE STAR OF SCHOLASTIC BRILLIANCE		
IF SELF ELEMENT IE. HEAVENLY STEM IN DAY PILLAR IS...	**AND EARTHLY BRANCH IN ANY PILLAR IS...**	
YANG WOOD		SNAKE - You have scholastic brilliance star
YIN WOOD		HORSE - You have scholastic brilliance star
YANG FIRE		MONKEY - You have scholastic brilliance star
YIN FIRE		ROOSTER - You have scholastic brilliance star
YANG EARTH		MONKEY - You have scholastic brilliance star
YIN EARTH		ROOSTER - You have scholastic brilliance star
YANG METAL		PIG - You have scholastic brilliance star
YIN METAL		RAT - You have scholastic brilliance star
YANG WATER		TIGER - You have scholastic brilliance star
YIN WATER		RABBIT - You have scholastic brilliance star

3 THE STAR OF AGGRESIVE SWORD

This star suggests a person who is intensive and aggressive all through life. This is a person who will emerge as some kind of champion for the underdog. At its most positive, the presence of this star suggests a powerful rebel leader, or a highly respected member of the opposition. Or it can be someone who seizes power by fair means or foul. The name of this star is *Yang Ren*, which describes yang essence (as in yin or yang) sharp blade that inflicts damage. This is a star that thus has great potential for good

or bad influences to materialize in one's life, but more negative than positive.

Whether this double-edged sword brings benefits or harm depends on whether its element is favourable or unfavorable to the Self-element. This star is favourable to a chart where the **self-element is weak**; then it will be excellent for bringing added confidence to the person thereby creating the cause for the attainment of great success.

Such a person will always stand up for the weak even when the odds are very much against winning; nevertheless he stays

BRANCH ELEMENTS TO INDICATE STAR OF AGGRESSIVE SWORD

IF SELF ELEMENT IE. HEAVENLY STEM IN DAY PILLAR IS...	AND EARTHLY BRANCH IN ANY PILLAR IS...	
YANG WOOD		RABBIT - You have aggressive sword star
YIN WOOD		TIGER - You have aggressive sword star
YANG FIRE		HORSE - You have aggressive sword star
YIN FIRE		SNAKE or SHEEP - You have aggressive sword starstar
YANG EARTH		HORSE - You have aggressive sword star
YIN EARTH		SNAKE - You have aggressive sword star
YANG METAL		ROOSTER - You have aggressive sword star
YIN METAL		MONKEY or DOG - You have aggressive sword star
YANG WATER		RAT - You have aggressive sword star
YIN WATER		PIG or OX - You have aggressive sword star

steadfast and strong willed. **Those who have this star will do very well as political leaders or as trade union bosses**. They have both the temperament and the staying power to become charismatic leaders. But they are also heavy handed and quick tempered. The star of the warrior sword indicates someone strong willed, determined and who does not suffer cowards or fools easily.

However take note that this star can be unfavorable in a chart where the self element is strong; That is when some kind of clash occurs making the person conceited, arrogant, overbearing and self centered. In instances where the elements clash the effect could even lead to bloodshed and violence.

Not everyone has the aggressive sword star in their *eight characters* chart. To determine if you have this star look at the **heavenly stem in your DAY pillar** (which is also your SELF element) and search for the required **earthly branch** in any of the four pillars. If the required combination of heavenly stem and earthly branch are present in the combinations indicated in the table were you are said to possess the aggressive sword approach to life.

Note that you can have as many as four aggressive sword stars and this is because there are 4 pillars. This will mean that your earthly branches will be the same animal sign and your self element is as indicated. Eg. If your self element is Yang wood, then each Rabbit in the earthly branch of any of the pillars will create a sword star. To feel the effects of this star all you need is a single star present in the chart. When you have too many sword stars it will turn you into such a fierce and quick-tempered person, no one will be able to reason with you. There is just too much wrath inside you.

* Additional information;

1. If the earthly branch is in the HOUR pillar it signifies that relationships with your children will have problems. It also indicates that there could be risk of coming under the surgeon's knife in your old age.

2. If the earthly branch is in the DAY pillar it signifies that there will be many petty squabbles with your spouse and a great deal of intolerance. It also signifies that your spouse constantly falls ill. The star is thus harmful to the spouse. It also suggests separation or divorce.

3. If the earthly branch is in the MONTH pillar, it signifies the person concerned will be very aggressive and if the element is unfavorable to the self element it suggests that the person is eccentric, bad tempered and strongly disliked.

4. If the earthly branch is in the YEAR pillar it signifies squabbles with the older patriarch of the family and can also indicate a squandering of family wealth.

4 THE STAR OF PROSPECTS

If you possess this star of prospects, and it is favourable to your self-element, you will possess the competitive edge in any field of endeavour you carve out a name for yourself. You have the determination, the staying power and the passion to succeed, and indeed you do succeed very well in your chosen profession.

Those who discover this star in their eight characters chart and its element is favourable to a weak self-element, the star causes strong determination that leads to success. There is nothing that cannot be achieved then, and success will come to them after much hard work. To them work is not a chore. Here we see the hand of ambition play a big role in this person's attainments. Usually the presence of this

BRANCH ELEMENTS TO INDICATE THE STAR OF PROSPECTS	
IF SELF ELEMENT IE. HEAVENLY STEM IN DAY PILLAR IS...	**AND EARTHLY BRANCH IN ANY PILLAR IS...**
YANG WOOD	TIGER - You have the star of Prospects
YIN WOOD	RABBIT - You have the star of Prospects
YANG FIRE	SNAKE - You have the star of Prospects
YIN FIRE	HORSE - You have the star of Prospects
YANG EARTH	SNAKE - You have the star of Prospects
YIN EARTH	HORSE - You have the star of Prospects
YANG METAL	MONKEY - You have the star of Prospects
YIN METAL	ROOSTER - You have the star of Prospects
YANG WATER	PIG - You have the star of Prospects
YIN WATER	RAT - You have the star of Prospects

star also suggests financial aid from friends and relatives during times of need but for this to occur there must not be a clash of elements between the branches of the different pillars.

Not everyone has the star of prospects in their eight characters chart. To determine if you have this star look at the **heavenly stem in your DAY pillar** (which is also your SELF element) and search for the required **earthly branch** in any of the four pillars. If the required combination of heavenly stem and earthly branch are present in the following combinations you are said to possess the star of prospects. You are a very willful and determined person seldom allowing anyone or anything to stand in your way

Note that you can have as many as four Prospects stars and this is because there are 4 pillars. This will mean that your earthly branches will be the same animal sign and your self-element is as indicated. Eg. If your self element is Yang WATER, then each PIG in the earthly branch of any of the pillars will create a determination star. To benefit form this star all you need is a single star present in the chart. When you have too many stars of Prospects it can make you an impossible person to live with, as you will be too obsessed with wanting to be a success.

5 THE STAR OF PEACH BLOSSOM

Some experts refer to this as the romance star, which indicates a person whose disposition is sweet and loving, and appear extremely attractive to the opposite sex. In a man the presence of this star in the chart indicates someone sexually desirable who can be very seductive. He is usually a ladies man.

In a woman this star indicates someone sexually irresistible. Women with this star will have little difficulty finding themselves a suitable husband – there will be many who will solicit her hand in marriage. In both genders the presence of this star always suggest someone who is socially popular and attractive.

Not everyone is blessed with the peach blossom star of love and romance in their *eight characters* chart. To determine if you have this star look at the **heavenly stem in your DAY pillar** (which is also your SELF element) and search for the required **earthly branch** in any of the four pillars. If the required combination of heavenly stem and earthly branch are present in the following combinations you are said to possess the peach blossom star.

Note that you can have as many as four PEACH BLOSSOM stars and this is because there are 4 pillars. This will mean that your earthly branches will be the

BRANCH ELEMENTS TO INDICATE THE PEACH BLOSSOM STAR

IF SELF ELEMENT IE. HEAVENLY STEM IN DAY PILLAR IS...	AND EARTHLY BRANCH IN ANY PILLAR IS...
YANG WOOD	HORSE - You have the peach blossom star
YIN WOOD	HORSE - You have the peach blossom star
YANG FIRE	RABBIT - You have the peach blossom star
YIN FIRE	SHEEP - You have the peach blossom star
YANG EARTH	DRAGON - You have the peach blossom star
YIN EARTH	DRAGON - You have the peach blossom star
YANG METAL	DOG - You have the peach blossom star
YIN METAL	ROOSTER - You have the peach blossom star
YANG WATER	RAT - You have the peach blossom star
YIN WATER	MONKEY - You have the peach blossom star

same animal sign and your self-element is as indicated. Eg. If your self element is Yang Metal, then each DOG in the earthly branch of any of the pillars will create a peach blossom star. To benefit from this star all you need is a single star present in the chart. When you have too many peach blossom stars it suggests that you are a good time person, rather cheaply seductive. In women it suggests you could be a courtesan.

6 FLOWER OF ROMANCE

The flower of romance is sometimes confused with the peach blossom star because it addresses the destiny of love. When the flower of romance is present in the eight characters chart, it suggests that there is genuine love and caring between husband and wife. But this is a star, which also reveals the occurrence of extra marital affairs. The differentiation is made between *internal romance* and *external romance* with the latter implying the occurrence of infidelity. If this is indicated in a woman's chart it means the husband will be unfaithful and if it occurs in a man's chart it suggests that the wife will be the one straying beyond the boundaries of marriage.

To determine if you have the Flower of romance star, look at the **earthly branch** **in your DAY or YEAR pillar** after which check if you have the animal sign that signifies the romance star. If the animal sign appears in the MONTH Pillar it signifies you have internal romance star luck, which means you have a loving relationship with your spouse. If it appears in the HOUR pillar it signifies the external romance star. This suggests there will be infidelity in your marriage.

BRANCH ELEMENTS TO INDICATE THE FLOWER OF ROMANCE

IF EARTHLY BRANCH IN DAY OR YEAR PILLAR IS:	EARTHLY BRANCH IN THE MONTH PILLAR SIGNIFIES INTERNAL ROMANCE AND IN THE HOUR PILLAR IT SIGNIFIES EXTERNAL ROMANCE I.E. INFIDELITY
RAT	ROOSTER - You have the flower romance star
OX	HORSE - You have the flower romance star
TIGER	RABBIT - You have the flower romance star
RABBIT	RAT - You have the flower romance star
DRAGON	ROOSTER - You have the flower romance star
SNAKE	HORSE - You have the flower romance star
HORSE	RABBIT - You have the flower romance star
SHEEP	RAT - You have the flower romance star
MONKEY	ROOSTER - You have the flower romance star
ROOSTER	HORSE - You have the flower romance star
DOG	RABBIT - You have the flower romance star
PIG	RAT - You have the flower romance star

INFIDELITY

Infidelity can also be counter checked by examining whether the Earthly Branch of the DAY pillar is clashing with any of the other Earthly Branches. This refers to the 6 kinds of clashes i.e. between rat and horse; sheep and ox; monkey and tiger; rooster and rabbit; dragon and dog; pig and snake. When the clash is coming from the MONTH or HOUR pillar it is most serious. It suggests the infidelity can lead to divorce especially if the person is going through a luck period when the elements are unfavorable.

7 THE COMMANDING STAR

This is an outstandingly auspicious star to have in the chart of an ambitious person as it indicates authority, power and influence a plenty. In Chinese this star is named *Jiang Sin*, or *commanding star*. If you have such a star in your chart it suggests that you definitely stand out in any crowd being born with a powerful disposition and a commanding presence. You have charisma and come across as someone very courageous, the stuff of heroes.

BRANCH ELEMENTS THAT INDICATE COMMANDING STAR

IF EARTHLY BRANCH IN THE DAY OR YEAR PILLAR IS:	AND EARTHLY BRANCH IN THE HOUR PILLAR IS...
RAT	RAT - You have the Commanding star
OX	ROOSTER - You have the Commanding star
TIGER	HORSE - You have the Commanding star
RABBIT	RABBIT - You have the Commanding star
DRAGON	RAT - You have the Commanding star
SNAKE	ROOSTER - You have the Commanding star
HORSE	HORSE - You have the Commanding star
SHEEP	RABBIT - You have the Commanding star
MONKEY	RAT - You have the Commanding star
ROOSTER	ROOSTER - You have the Commanding star
DOG	HORSE - You have the Commanding star
PIG	RABBIT - You have the Commanding star

You will possess the easy authority of someone *born to rule*. You will have wealth and many followers; people look up to you and expect you to have leadership qualities. Even when you do not demonstrate much promise as a child, you will emerge as a powerful leader in later years. Exactly when this trait shows itself depends on the elements of your ten year luck pillars. Look for the periods when your favourable elements make an appearance. In the modern context such a person could well be powerful political leader or a CEO of a mighty multinational corporation. Or it can be a minister of a country.

While this is an excellent star to have in the chart, if its signifying element in the HOUR pillar is unfavorable to the Self element of the chart, then from being an auspicious star it becomes a harmful star bringing severe harm and obstacles into the life of the person. It is thus a very formidable star and one, which must be closely monitored.

Not everyone is blessed with the Commanding star of power and authority in their *eight characters* chart. To determine if you have this star look at the **earthly branch in your DAY or YEAR pillar** and search for the required **earthly branch** in the HOUR pillar as indicated. If the required combination of earthly branches is present in the following combinations you are said to possess the Commanding star.

Note that here we are looking at the animal signs or Earthly Branches of three of the Pillars in the *eight characters* chart. Here we look at the DAY and YEAR pillars first and check what the animal sign of these pillars are, and then from there we proceed to check the HOUR Pillar for the "correct" animal sign that will indicate the presence of this much coveted Commanding star. For example if your YEAR or DAY animal sign is MONKEY then what you need is a RAT in your HOUR Pillar – then you are blessed with the Commanding star. Then you need to pray that the element is favourable for your self element.

8 THE STAR OF THE TRAVELLING HORSE

As its name suggests this star is associated with traveling luck. If you have such a star in your chart it means you have the luck to travel far and wide beyond your shores. It also means that you could work overseas far from home for long periods of time. It is generally regarded as an auspicious star to possess. However when it clashes with any of the other stars mentioned in this chapter it has the power to destroy the good fortune indicated by the other star, and create misfortune in its stead so in some ways this can be a dangerous star to have.

And when it meets up with a troublesome and aggravating star such as one of the aggressive stars - WARRIOR STAR or WAR STAR - it will make matters even worse. A clash takes place when there are other

BRANCH ELEMENTS TO INDICATE THE TRAVELLING HORSE STAR

IF EARTHLY BRANCH IN THE DAY OR YEAR PILLAR IS:	AND EARTHLY BRANCH IN THE HOUR PILLAR IS...
RAT	TIGER - You have the Traveling Horse star
OX	PIG - You have the Traveling Horse star
TIGER	MONKEY - You have the Traveling Horse star
RABBIT	SNAKE - You have the Traveling Horse star
DRAGON	TIGER - You have the Traveling Horse star
SNAKE	PIG - You have the Traveling Horse star
HORSE	MONKEY - You have the Traveling Horse star
SHEEP	SNAKE - You have the Traveling Horse star
MONKEY	TIGER - You have the Traveling Horse star
ROOSTER	PIG - You have the Travelling Horse star
DOG	MONKEY - You have the Traveling Horse star
PIG	SNAKE - You have the Traveling Horse star

good stars in your chart. The closer the star is to the traveling horse star the greater the damage to that other "good" star. Hence this is rather a dangerous star to have. Like the Horse it is named after, when it takes off, it could well be galloping so fast you cannot stop and the outcome could be disaster. It can also cause havoc when its element clashes with another element in a nearby pillar.

So it is perhaps not a bad thing that not everyone is blessed with the traveling horse star in their *eight characters* chart. If you have too many of this star in your chart it suggests an unsettled life marked by frequent travels that disrupts family life and happiness.

To determine if you have this star, look at the **earthly branch in your DAY or YEAR**

pillar and search for the required **earthly branch** in the HOUR pillar as indicated in the table on page 116.

Note that here we are looking first at the animal signs or earthly branches of two of the Pillars in the *eight characters* chart ie. the DAY and YEAR pillars. Check what the animal sign of these pillars are, and from there proceed to check the HOUR Pillar for the animal sign that will indicate the presence of the Traveling Horse star in your chart. For example if your YEAR or DAY animal sign is RAT then what you need is a TIGER in your HOUR Pillar − to indicate you have the Traveling Horse star.

BRANCH ELEMENTS TO INDICATE THE SPIRITUAL STAR

IF EARTHLY BRANCH IN THE DAY OR YEAR PILLAR IS:	AND EARTHLY BRANCH IN THE HOUR PILLAR IS...
RAT	DRAGON - You have the Spiritual star
OX	OX - You have the Spiritual star
TIGER	DOG - You have the Spiritual star
RABBIT	SHEEP - You have the Spiritual star
DRAGON	DRAGON - You have the Spiritual star
SNAKE	OX - You have the Spiritual star
HORSE	DOG - You have the Spiritual star
SHEEP	SHEEP - You have the Spiritual star
MONKEY	DRAGON - You have the Spiritual star
ROOSTER	OX - You have the Spiritual star
DOG	DOG - You have the Spiritual star
PIG	SHEEP - You have the Spiritual star

9 STAR OF SPIRITUALITY

The presence of this star of spirituality in you chart suggests you could be a philosopher someone who enjoys thinking and developing the mind. You are definitely not much of a social person as you prefer your own company and the silence of quiet meditation.

The experts also point to this star to indicate a leaning towards the spiritual life and even that it could lead to this person becoming a monk or a nun. Such a person is usually of course a very spiritual person. If you have this star in your chart, you have the destiny to lead a deeply religious life or even a hermit's existence.

To determine if you have this star, look at the earthly branch in your DAY or YEAR pillar in the table on page 117 and search for the required **earthly branch in the HOUR pillar** as indicated. If the required combination of **earthly branches** is present in the combinations indicated possess the star of Spirituality.

Note that here we are looking at the animal signs or earthly branches of three of the Pillars in the *eight characters* chart. Here we look at the DAY and YEAR pillars first and check what the animal sign of these pillars are, and then from there we proceed to check the HOUR Pillar for the "correct" animal sign that will indicate the presence of the Spiritual star in your chart. For example if your YEAR or DAY animal sign is HORSE then if you have a DOG in your HOUR Pillar – it indicates you have the Spiritual star.

10 THE WAR STAR

This is akin to the General fighting a war and wins with good strategy and foresight. The presence of the War Star suggests a person of high intellect with great ability in planning and strategic defense. This is one smart person, someone crafty and elusive and who is able to play many roles like a chameleon. In its most positive and favourable manifestation the presence of this star implies someone who can rise high up in the hierarchy of a country's defense. It is a star that suggests someone who commands an army. But this is also a star that can turn unfavorable. For instance when it is overshadowed by the Traveling Horse star. When it becomes inauspicious this star brings robbery luck.

To determine if you have this star, look at the **earthly branch in your DAY or YEAR pillar** and search for the required **earthly branch** in the HOUR pillar as indicated in the table on page 119.

If the required combination of earthly branches is present in the combinations indicated, you possess the War Star.

BRANCH ELEMENTS TO INDICATE THE WAR STAR

IF EARTHLY BRANCH IN THE DAY OR YEAR PILLAR IS:	AND EARTHLY BRANCH IN THE HOUR PILLAR IS...
RAT	SNAKE - You have the War star
OX	TIGER - You have the War star
TIGER	PIG - You have the War star
RABBIT	MONKEY - You have the War star
DRAGON	SNAKE - You have the War star
SNAKE	TIGER - You have the War star
HORSE	PIG - You have the War star
SHEEP	MONKEY - You have the War star
MONKEY	SNAKE - You have the War star
ROOSTER	TIGER - You have the War star
DOG	PIG - You have the War star
PIG	MONKEY - You have the War star

Note that here we are looking at the animal signs or earthly branches of three of the Pillars in the *eight characters* chart. First we look at the DAY and YEAR pillars and check what the animal sign of these pillars are, from there we check the HOUR Pillar for the animal sign that indicate the presence of the WAR star in your chart. For example if your YEAR or DAY animal sign is ROOSTER then if you have a TIGER in your HOUR Pillar − it indicates you have the WAR star, you are someone exceedingly skilled in the art of war and the use of strategy.

11 THE WARRIOR STAR

This star is also referred to as the Death star although its presence in the chart is nowhere near as foreboding. The warrior star, suggests a brave and courageous person, ever eager to fight for a Course. The presence of this star in the chart indicates someone ever ready to fight against the injustice of the world. If it is overshadowed in any way by the presence of the Traveling Horse star this warrior star will attract court

BRANCH ELEMENTS TO INDICATE WARRIOR STAR

IF EARTHLY BRANCH DAY OR YEAR PILLARS IS:	AND EARTHLY BRANCH IN THE HOUR PILLAR IS...
RAT	PIG - You have the Warrior star
OX	MONKEY - You have the Warrior star
TIGER	SNAKE - You have the Warrior star
RABBIT	TIGER - You have the Warrior star
DRAGON	PIG - You have the Warrior star
SNAKE	MONKEY - You have the Warrior star
HORSE	SNAKE - You have the Warrior star
SHEEP	TIGER - You have the Warrior star
MONKEY	PIG - You have the Warrior star
ROOSTER	MONKEY - You have the Warrior star
DOG	SNAKE - You have the Warrior star
PIG	TIGER - You have the Warrior star

cases, litigations and also great misfortune to one's spouse. This star is thus to be viewed rather suspiciously. To overcome the effects of this star it is necessary to use the element cures to suppress the HOUR earthly branch element.

To determine if you have the Warrior star, look at the **earthly branch in your DAY or YEAR pillar** and search for the required **earthly branch** in the HOUR pillar as indicated in the table above. If the required combination of earthly branches are present in the combinations shown you possess the Warrior Star.

Here we are looking once more, at the animal signs or earthly branches of three of the Pillars in the *eight characters* chart. We look at the DAY and YEAR pillars first and check what the animal sign of these pillars are, and then from there we proceed to check the HOUR Pillar for the animal sign that will indicate the presence of the WARRIOR star in your chart. For example if your YEAR or DAY animal sign is SNAKE then if you have a MONKEY in your HOUR Pillar – it indicates you have the WARRIOR star, you are someone exceedingly brave and courageous.

THE ELEMENTS THAT INDICATE
THE STAR OF POWERFUL MENTORS

IF EARTHLY BRANCH IN THE DAY OR YEAR PILLAR IS:	CHECK IF THE EARTHLY BRANCH OR HEAVENLY STEM INDICATED BELOW IS PRESENT IN THE REST OF THE CHART
RAT	EARTHLY BRANCH SNAKE
OX	HEAVENLY STEM YANG METAL
TIGER	HEAVENLY STEM YIN FIRE
RABBIT	EARTHLY BRANCH MONKEY
DRAGON	HEAVENLY STEM YANG WATER
SNAKE	HEAVENLY STEM YIN METAL
HORSE	EARTHLY BRANCH PIG
SHEEP	HEAVENLY STEM YANG WOOD
MONKEY	HEAVENLY STEM YIN WATER
ROOSTER	EARTHLY BRANCH TIGER
DOG	HEAVENLY STEM YANG FIRE
PIG	HEAVENLY STEM YIN WOOD

THE STAR OF POWERFUL MENTORS

This is one of the more auspicious "stars" that you can have in your paht chee chart because when it is present it is like having a fairy godmother or a guardian angel always watching you over your shoulders. To the Chinese, mentor luck used to always imply the assistance of a powerful father figure whose wise counsel guides along the career of a younger person. In modern times of course, the presence of mentors no longer has a gender bias. So when this star is present, your powerful mentor can be a man or a woman. Note that when one has a "patron" who plays the role of a mentor in one's life, the person need not be an obvious figure. Often mentors work discreetly but very effectively in the background.

12 THE STAR OF POWERFUL MENTORS

In Chinese destiny analysis much is made of "mentor" luck, which in the old days was often the main success factor in the career of young scholars hoping to enjoy patronage in the Court of the Emperor. In modern times it is just as excellent to enjoy the luck of being supported, helped and guided by powerful benefactors. Indeed success often comes from "who you know rather than what you know."

In the *eight characters* chart, the appearance of powerful benefactors or patrons in one's life is indicated by the presence of the *powerful mentors star* which is sometimes also referred to as the *heavenly virtue star*. When this star is present in your eight characters chart it indicates that you will always have someone powerful to help you succeed, and during times of danger there will always be someone there to help you.

To detect the presence of the powerful Mentors star check the table on the previous page. First note the earthly branch in your MONTH Pillar; then check the rest of the chart to see if the indicated *earthly branch* or *heavenly stem* appears in either the YEAR, MONTH, DAY or HOUR Pillars ie in the rest of the chart.

INTREPRETING THE SYMBOLIC STARS

The presence of any of the stars covered in this Chapter suggests the potential for the indicated good/ bad fortune to create additional influences in your life. However these indications should always be read within the larger framework of the chart as well as the ten year luck pillars.

At all times it is important to remember that whatever is "missing" from the chart indicates a weakness, which prevents the manifestation of good fortune. It is always necessary to ensure that whatever is missing is compensated for in some way or another.

One should also never ignore the favourable and unfavorable elements that make up the preliminary readings of the chart since these are the fundamental underpinnings of the strength of the chart. Elements of each of the successive years is also important in their impact on one's *eight characters* chart.

Part Six

INCORPORATING CHINESE ASTROLOGY

INCORPORATING CHINESE ASTROLOGY

*E*ight characters chart readings should be supplemented with Chinese astrological readings each year so that destiny analysis stays updated. This is because astrological forces have a major impact on good and bad luck days. Reading the effect of chi energy changes that take place every year are considerably more accurate when the birth details as reflected in the four pillars are used to create the paht chee chart.

This dimension of luck improvements focus on the effect which different days, months and years have on personal forecast luck and therefore success potential.

The passage of time i.e. different year and months can also bring afflictions and dangers, which unless avoided or remedied can manifest misfortunes such as illness, accidents, setbacks and problems into one's life. Time dimension changes in one's fortunes fall broadly under the umbrella of Chinese astrology whose origins are derived from the cosmic turtle and the 12 animal signs that signify one's year of birth based on the lunar calendar.

In the *eight characters* chart the animal sign is the *earthly branch* character of the YEAR pillar. In Chinese astrology the animal signs have additional connotations and attributes that offer extra information. These complement the readings of the eight

characters chart and its accompanying luck pillars. You can use your animal sign based on your year of birth to compile additional information that can reveal **near term** indications of impending great good fortune. Or impending misfortunes.

Chinese astrology also reveal dangerous afflictions such as illness, accidents, loss and other probable manifestations of bad luck in any year that might befall you, and here is where the **preventive dimension of Chinese Personal Forecasting** is so wonderful. As they say, being forewarned is being fore armed. When you know when a certain year threatens to be a misfortune year, it is actually possible to take precautionary measures based on element cures and remedies. This is why Chinese astrology can be so awesome when used in conjunction with one's paht chee.

THE ASTROLOGY WHEEL & PLANET JUPITER

*I*n Chinese astrology the twelve animals signs are part of the 24 compass directions. Each animal sign occupies alternate fifteen degrees of the compass and this corresponds to "the flight path of the planet Jupiter."

Jupiter is one of the nine planets of our solar system. Its size is beyond imagination. Jupiter's mass is far greater than the sum of the other planets combined. Its volume is 1,400 times that of the earth. Not only is it the largest planet, it is also the fastest planet and it's radiation is greater than that of the sun! Jupiter is thus a powerful and influential influence. To ancient Romans, Jupiter was an important planet. They regarded Jupiter as the leader of their pantheon of Gods. To them Jupiter was the "God of the Universe". Orientals as well as Occidentals thus acknowledge Jupiter's influence. To the Chinese, Jupiter is the God of each year.

THE SIGNIFICANCE OF THE NUMBER TWELVE

According to astronomical evidence Jupiter has twelve satellites and it takes twelve years to complete one full orbit around the sun. The number twelve is thus very significant as it coincides with the Chinese system of having twelve animal signs signify the twelve *earthly branches* of their calendar. The twelve Chinese Zodiac signs that are placed around the compass also indicates the location of the planet Jupiter in each of the twelve years.

TAI SUI

In Chinese this planet is known as the Tai Sui and it exerts different kinds of influences on people's destiny according to their animal sign. The planet Jupiter takes the equivalent of one Chinese year to move fifteen degrees of the compass.

In any year therefore Jupiter or Tai Sui resides in the direction that corresponds to the animal sign of the year. The Tai Sui in Chinese astrology and feng shui is thus located by looking at the angle that corresponds to that of the animal sign in any given year.

For example the year 2005 is a Rooster year so Tai Sui is residing in the West as this is the direction of the Rooster. In 2006, the Tai Sui will have moved to the Northwest 1, specifically the location of the Dog and in so doing changes the energies of the new year.

The Chinese regard the Tai Sui as the "God of the year". Some describe him as the Commander in chief of the Gods and from ancient times Tai Sui has been regarded as the most powerful of the "Earth Deities". In the old days, the Chinese called it the "Sui Star" or "Year Star.".

From those times they believed that the planets and stars exerted great influence on phenomena on earth, and on men's fortunes, while moving along their orbital paths. They believed for instance that the moon affects the tides of the oceans and subliminally influences human behavior.

Classical experts of the Chinese astrological sciences intone that "*the Tai Sui can sit but he cannot be confronted.*" Nothing brings better fortune than cultivating the Tai Sui and nothing brings greater misfortune than offending and confronting the Tai Sui.

> **So, notwithstanding what one's birth charts may be predicting for us, on a near term basis it is vitally important to take note of the astrological forces of every given year and follow the taboos associated with the astrological afflictions. One of these is the Tai Sui.**

SITTING AND CULTIVATING THE TAI SUI

means undertaking constructive and *productive* activities in the direction where the Tai Sui is located in any particular year. This includes undertaking construction work, repairing as well as renovating. Some practitioners also include moving house starting from the Tai Sui location as being auspicious. Or planting a tree if the Tai Sui direction happens to fall in the wood directions of east and southeast; installing a new light when it moves to the south; creating a small mound of earth when it occupies the southwest, and northeast, and installing a small water feature in the north.

When the Tai Sui is in the west or northwest it is a good idea to place windchimes or other auspicious images (especially the Pi Yao) made of metal there. When you respect the Tai Sui, it rewards you with success and good fortune. This becomes especially important for those born in the animal sign of the year.

For example in 2005, the Tai Sui occupies the west, the place of the Rooster so those born in rooster years should undertake productive activities in the west to enjoy the powerful good luck brought by Tai Sui. Those born in other animal years should likewise tap the west direction in the same manner. In 2006 the Tai Sui moves to the location of the Dog, which occupies the Northwest. Thus, by simply observing the Tai Sui's location it is possible to benefit from knowledge of Chinese astrology.

FACING OR OFFENDING THE TAI SUI

means engaging in destructive activities in the Tai Sui's location. This includes demolishing work, digging a pond or digging a hole. So for those thinking of undertaking renovations in the Tai Sui locations, doing so would have adverse effects on those living in the home where this occurs. This is because almost all renovation work involves some demolishing work. Some say that even chopping down a tree (especially when the Tai Sui is in the East or Southeast) in the Tai Sui's direction is offending the Tai Sui and this can lead to pretty grave misfortunes.

> **"When Tai Sui sits above your head, there is no happiness and only calamity will occur. When Tai Sui appears to confront your animal sign, even if you are healthy, you may encounter financial loss."**

Here is a graphic, which shows the location of the animal signs and thus the place where the Tai Sui will be over the next twelve years.

THE ASTROLOGY WHEEL

SHOWING THE
LOCATION
OF THE TAI SUI ON
THE COMPASS IN
DIFFERENT YEARS

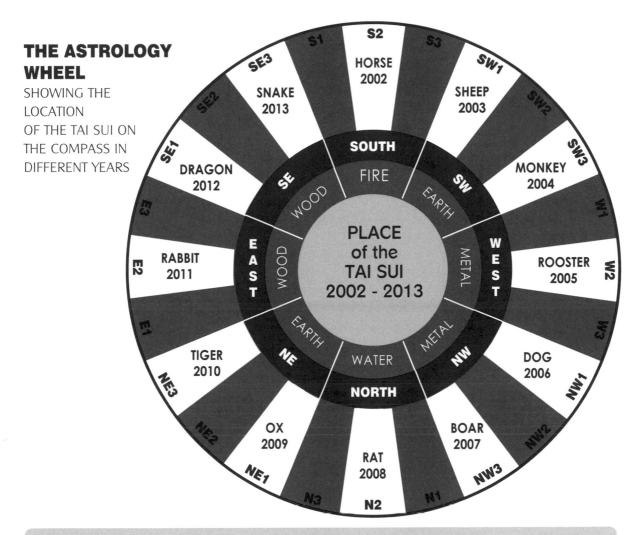

This Astrology wheel illustrates the 24 sub directions of fifteen degrees each, that make up the 360 degrees of the compass. The Chinese refer to these sub-directions as the "24 mountains" of the compass. The Earthly branches i.e. the 12 animal signs occupy each alternate sub-direction (as illustrated above) so they are regarded as being part of the 24 mountains in compass formula feng shui. Note that each direction has its own element and this is not always the same element as that of the animal sign. In paht chee analysis we consider the intrinsic element of the animal sign and NOT the element of the location they occupy when we interpret the charts. Meanwhile note that the TAI SUI or GOD OF THE YEAR is located in the compass sub-direction of the animal sign, when that animal sign rules the year. eg in 2006, the year of the Rooster, the TAI SUI was located in the place of the Rooster which is West.

ANNUAL READINGS OF LUCK BASED ON ANIMAL SIGNS

*O*f greater significance to one's fortunes is the study of the impact of the year's forces on the personal forecasts of one's luck for any particular year based on one's animal sign. There are potent ways to unlocking the secrets of the luck of the year, and the method that offers the most comprehensive details of one's annual luck are the numbers of the Lo Shu magic square. By their positioning in each different year, the nine numbers of the Lo Shu square unlocks a great deal of vital information which can be incorporated into one's personal forecasts for that year. All the afflictions can be noted and systematically neutralized while auspicious indications can be taken advantage of.

ANNUAL LO SHU CHARTS

*I*n each year a different Lo Shu chart "rules" the fortunes of the different directions as well as the different animal signs. The Lo Shu chart in every year is derived by the designated Lo Shu number of the year and these are extracted from the Chinese thousand-year calendar. According to this calendar the Lo Shu number of the year 2005 is 4 and that of 2006 is 3. The Lo Shu chart for 2005 and 2006 are thus derived with the numbers 4 and 3 in the center. The other numbers between 1 to 9 are entered into the Lo shu three grid by three grid square. Using the same sequential arrangemnt of numbers. The two charts for 2005 and 2006 are below as drawn:

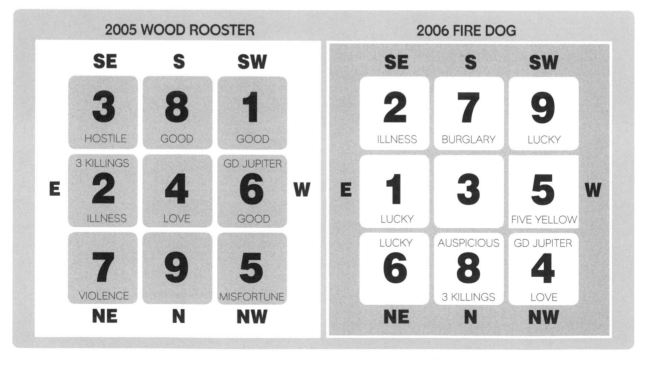

2005 WOOD ROOSTER

SE	S	SW
3 HOSTILE	**8** GOOD	**1** GOOD
3 KILLINGS **2** ILLNESS	**4** LOVE	GD JUPITER **6** GOOD
7 VIOLENCE	**9**	**5** MISFORTUNE

E / W

NE / N / NW

2006 FIRE DOG

SE	S	SW
2 ILLNESS	**7** BURGLARY	**9** LUCKY
1 LUCKY	**3**	**5** FIVE YELLOW
LUCKY **6**	AUSPICIOUS **8** 3 KILLINGS	GD JUPITER **4** LOVE

E / W

NE / N / NW

Note how the rest of the numbers are filled into the square after the center number has been determined. These annual charts reveal a great deal of information about the year as well as about the outlook for individuals based on their animal sign. The key is to be able to read how each of the directional locations are affected by the characteristics and attributes of each of the nine different numbers that "fly" into the direction during the year. For example the lucky number 8 brings good luck to the South location in 2005 and because the South is also the horse location, those born in the horse years will enjoy good fortune in 2005. Likewise in the year 2006 the lucky 8 will fly to the North and this means that the North enjoys exceptional good luck in 2006. Since this is also the location of the Rat born person, the year 2006 is said to bring exceptional good fortune for the Rat. It is important to know how to draw up the annual Lo Shu chart to undertake annual readings for different people born under different signs of the Chinese Zodiac. To do this all you need to know is the Lo shu number for the year.

HERE ARE THE LO SHU NUMBERS FOR DIFFERENT YEARS

YEAR	REIGNING NUMBER	YEAR	REIGNING NUMBER
2005	4	2018	9
2006	3	2019	8
2007	2	2020	7
2008	1	2021	6
2009	9	2022	5
2010	8	2023	4
2011	7	2024	3
2012	6	2025	2
2013	5	2026	1
2014	4	2027	9
2015	3	2028	8
2016	2	2029	7
2017	1	2030	6

MONTHLY LO SHU CHARTS

In addition to the annual charts it is also possible to draw up the Lo Shu charts for each of the calendar months of the year. In this context do take note that the annual as well as monthly charts are based on the HSIA or solar calendar of the Chinese system of measuring time. The Chinese have two calendars, a lunar calendar as well as a HSIA calendar. To interpret Chinese astrology we use the HSIA calendar. However for paht chee readings and to determine one's animal sign we use the lunar calendar.

Each month as defined by the HSIA calendar there will be a ruling number and this number becomes the center number of the ruling Lo Shu chart for that month. To draw the monthly chart therefore and place the numbers correctly around the nine grid chart all one needs to be familiar with is the flight of the stars. This enables us to place the rest of the numbers 1 to 9 around the Lo Shu square. Reading the meanings of the numbers in the monthly and annual charts require us to know the meanings of the individual numbers as well as combinations of numbers. Each number has a different meaning and each number also has an element associated with it. Using the meanings of the numbers as well as the effect of the elements combining with the elements of one's animal sign we reveals personal forecast luck of each of the months. Use the Tables in the preceding

THE NUMBERS BELOW REPRESENT THE LO SHU NUMBERS OF THE MONTHS

CHINESE MONTH	START OF MONTH	YEAR OF RAT, RABBIT, HORSE & ROOSTER	YEAR OF DOG, DRAGON, OX & SHEEP	YEAR OF TIGER, PIG, SNAKE & MONKEY
1	FEB 4TH	8	5	2
2	MARCH 6TH	7	4	1
3	APRIL 5TH	6	3	9
4	MAY 6TH	5	2	8
5	JUNE 6TH	4	1	7
6	JULY 7TH	3	9	6
7	AUGUST 8TH	2	8	5
8	SEPTEMBER 8TH	1	7	4
9	OCTOBER 8TH	9	6	3
10	NOVEMBER 7TH	8	5	2
11	DECEMBER 7TH	7	4	1
12	JANUARY 6TH	6	3	9

Note: The above is the summary of the 10,000 year calendar

paper to determine the Lo shu numbers of the different months and years. These tables are based on the HSIA calendar and they can also be used to check western calendar dates that demarcate the Chinese months.

MEANINGS OF THE LO SHU NUMBERS

For purposes of determining the luck prospects of individuals you need to first determine the compass location of your animal sign. Thus if you are born in the year of the rooster, your fortunes will be affected by the numbers that fly to your direction West. It is thus important to know what the numbers mean.

1, 6, 8

As a general rule the numbers 1, 6 and 8 being the white numbers are deemed to be extremely auspicious – with the 8 being the most auspicious as we are now in the period of 8. This number 8 is an earth number so its effect on different directions will be different. Generally speaking they will exhaust the South sector and bring good fortune to the NW and West sectors.

The number 1 indicates career success and it belongs to the water element. It thus brings excellent luck to the east and Southeast sector animal signs. The number 6 belongs to the metal element and it brings excellent good fortune to the Rat born person

OTHER GOOD LUCK NUMBERS

The number 4 brings the luck of romance and literary endeavours while the number 9 is a magnifying number seriously expanding your good luck whenever it is accompanied and strengthened by a powerful good fortune star such as 1, 6 or 8.

2, 5, 3, 7

The danger numbers are 2 and 5 which brings illness and loss respectively. The number 3 brings quarrelsome vibes, court cases and aggravations. The number 7 brings burglary and violence. When the numbers are doubled they indicate the concept of double goodness of double trouble depending on what numbers they are. Chinese astrology always starts from an analysis of the Lo Shu numbers that affect one's luck during the months of any year. It is very useful knowing what the numbers affecting us are indicating since they offer valuable signposts and signals to what lies in store in any given year. When you are aware of the afflictions of the year you can install cures and when you are on a roll you will likewise know how beneficial it might be to be courageous in that year.

Indeed, knowing with a certain amount of confidence what lies in store in any given year enables us to make better living & investment decisions and with greater confidence. Chinese astrology then becomes a valuable tool for living and working.

THE LO SHU NUMBER OF THE DAY

As with the month and the year, each day is also associated with a lo shu number. Like the numbers of the year and month these can be extracted from the Almanac calendar. In any case Lo shu numbers of the years, months and days follow a cyclical pattern and in the case of days, the Lo shu numbers follow the ascending order of White 1, Black 2, Blue 3, Green 4, Yellow 5, White 6, Red 7, White 8 and Purple 9. It is a simple enough matter to refer to the calendar for the Lo Shu number of the day to determine if a particular activity can be undertaken or avoided. This is summarized for each of the nine Lo Shu numbers:

WHITE 1 - when the Lo shu is 1 one should be extra careful with one's young children. They should not be allowed to run about outside the house as misfortune can befall them. But this number is excellent for bathing purification and making ritual offerings.

BLACK 2 - on this day it is a good idea not to stay out too late at night. Traveling at night is definitely advised against. This is also not a day to weep or cry, go swimming or take physical risks. This is a good day to perform rituals that cleanse the home so this is an excellent day to do spring cleaning and space clearing.

BLUE 3 - this is a bad day to cut trees - one should not disturb the wood element on this day. So best to avoid doing any work with plants and in the garden. It is also not a good idea to drive nails into wood today. Keep the home well lit on this day.

GREEN 4 - this is a day when one should not allow a young child out of the house. Better that the child stays indoors. His/her head should not be exposed to the skies. A widow should not wash her hair. It is a good day to seek medicinal cures for any of one's ailments.

YELLOW 5 - this is a day when one should not disturb the soil by digging, ploughing or sowing seeds. One should also not participate in festivals of invite a dog home. This is a good day for making petitions to the authorities and for undertaking all kinds of virtuous and charitable acts.

WHITE 6 - this is a day when one should keep complaints (whining and lamenting) to a minimum. It is a day when praising oneself and being arrogant would attract a great

deal of problems. Make a special effort to avoid people wanting to find fault with you. This is an excellent day for making petitions to the Gods and for praying.

RED 7 - this is NOT a day to cook red meat, eat meat or worst take animals to the slaughter. This can potentially be a violent day. One should also avoid using fire

WHITE 8 - this is a bad day to burn food or garbage or handle soiled objects. One should not mourn or weep as this will deplete one's vitality. It is a good day to get married, performs purification or attend prayer sessions.

PURPLE 9 – is NOT a day to trust anyone with a special mission or to send emissaries. You can lose a great deal of money from doing so. This is a good day to recover money owing to you.

GOOD & BAD DAYS FOR EACH OF THE ANIMAL SIGN

ach of the twelve animals signs of one's year of birth is also said to have an "excellent" day, as well as a day of great vitality. There is also a day of "obstructions". When the day of one's birth corresponds with these excellent and obstruction days there is a particular meaning for the individual. These good and bad days are derived by the influence of planets and for ease of reference I have summarized what these days are for each of the twelve animal signs in the Table below.

From the Table, take note of the three days that mean something for you. First remember never to undertake anything important on your day of obstacles. If you were born on your day of obstacle it is advisable to wear "cures" that overcome the unfavourable aspect of the planetary influence of that day. However take note of that day and avoid doing anything important on that day.

GOOD & BAD DAYS BASED ON YOUR ANIMAL SIGN

ANIMAL SIGN	EXCELLENT DAY	VITALITY DAY	OBSTACLE DAY
RAT	WEDNESDAY	TUESDAY	SATURDAY
OX	SATURDAY	WEDNESDAY	THURSDAY
TIGER	THURSDAY	SATURDAY	FRIDAY
RABBIT	THURSDAY	SATURDAY	FRIDAY
DRAGON	SUNDAY	WEDNESDAY	THURSDAY
SNAKE	TUESDAY	FRIDAY	WEDNESDAY
HORSE	TUESDAY	FRIDAY	WEDNESDAY
SHEEP	FRIDAY	WEDNESDAY	THURSDAY
MONKEY	FRIDAY	THURSDAY	TUESDAY
ROOSTER	FRIDAY	THURSDAY	TUESDAY
DOG	MONDAY	WEDNESDAY	THURSDAY
BOAR	WEDNESDAY	TUESDAY	SATURDAY

DAY OF OBSTACLES

*I*f your day of obstacle is Monday, note that this is deemed to be the day of the Moon, which is also referred to as the planet of the soul of women. If this is your day of obstacle note that you should not take leave of loved ones on this day, start a long journey, attend a funeral, or undertake any fire rituals. Avoid heavy exercise.

If your day of obstacle is Tuesday, this is the day of Mars also known as the planet of the soul of men. Definitely you should not get married on this day. Nor should you hire new employees, make contracts, sign new agreements or embark on a journey.

If your day of obstacles is a Wednesday, this is the day of Mercury, the planet of the soul of the prince. It is generally a positive day but for you, please avoid selling anything on this day. You should also not make offerings or gifts on this day and you should avoid going to see the doctor.

If your day of obstacle is a Thursday, it is the day of Jupiter, the planet of the Bodhisattva spirit. This is usually regarded as a spiritual day. For you it is advisable to take a peaceful stance on this day. Do not quarrel or start a fight with anyone. It is also not a good time to undertake construction work, build a roof or start anything negative on this day. It is a day when you must not do anything unkind to animals such as slaughtering or hunting them.

If your day of obstacle is a Friday, it is the day of Venus, also a day of magic power, a day of the soul of medicines. It is a day that should not be spent disputing with people or negotiating settlements with others. Anything violent on this day will attract dire consequences.

If your day of obstacle is Saturday, it is the day of Saturn and it is also referred to as the neutral day. For you Saturday is unfavourable for almost all kinds of activity so you should refrain from buying or selling anything, refrain from getting into arguments or fist fights with anyone and definitely you must refrain from building, starting a project, opening a shop or launching a new product. Do not go on a journey today and try not to visit friends or attend festivities.

If your day of obstacle is Sunday, it is the day of the sun, often referred to as the planet of the Gods. This is the planet of the royal soul and is usually an important day for members of royalty. For you however Sunday is unfavourable so you should not move house, change office, undertake surgical operations, embark on a journey attend a funeral, undertake any kind of gardening or planting activity and also refrain from celebrating your birthday, marriage or christening on a Sunday.

DAYS OF EXCELLENCE & VITALITY

If you were born on either your day of excellence or your day of vitality you are sure to be intelligent and extremely resourceful. Your life is filled with lucky signs and good omens. You will succeed easily in everything you undertake and it is likely that you will live a long and stable life. Your day of vitality will also be good days for you to undertake a large variety of activities and things move smoothly for you on these days. So check the Table and commit your day of vitality to memory.

Plan all your important occasions to take place on this day. The day of excellence is a day when your spiritual energy will be at its highest so this is a good day to meditate and chant special prayers. Your day of vitality is the day when your intrinsic vitality is at its highest point during the week. This is thus an excellent day to undertake any projects that require a high level of energy and a great deal of concentration.

If your day of vitality is Monday, it is the day of the planet Moon and this day is favourable for you to start new projects, sowing seeds, adopting children, buying and selling, celebrating festivals and improving the feng shui of your home. Any kind of space cleansing and purification activities will meet with great success.

If your day of vitality is Tuesday, it is the day of Mars and this is a day that is favourable for military type operations – any activity requiring military strategy and precision. Today is a good day for borrowing money, moving house, gambling, and taking risks. It is also a good day to make investments in the stock market.

If your day of vitality is Wednesday, it is a day of Mercury, and it is an excellent day to undertake interviews, make publicity, embark on a journey get married, and participate in any kind of celebrations. It is also an excellent day for completing unfinished work.

If your day of vitality is Thursday, it is a day of the powerfully spiritual planet Jupiter, a day favourable for undertaking activities with religious and spiritual aspirations. It is a good day to make offerings at temples, get married, start a study program, plant plants, sow seeds, prepare medicines study divination techniques and go horse riding. It is the kind of day which will attract new friends into your life and give your spirits a major lift.

If your day of vitality is Friday, it is a magical day which belongs to the great planet Venus. This is a day that favours you the teacher. It is great to indulge in generosity on this day, doing charity work, going for surgery, start a journey, prepare medicine, plant trees, and entering into an intimate relationship with someone for the first time.

If your day of vitality is Saturday, is a day of the planet Saturn so it is a rather lame day. But it is an excellent day to commence work on building a new house, move homes, transfer to another job, acquire a new pet, say long life prayers, and cleaning house. This is also a good day for starting a regime in exercising.

If your day of vitality is Sunday, this day of the sun makes you have affinity with those born into the royal houses of the world. Sunday is a day that is favourable to all your activities connected with celebrations. Marriage, birthdays and other occasions of celebration are blessed on this day for you. It is not a day to work but rather a day to enjoy the pleasures of your world.

AUSPICIOUS DAYS OF THE MONTH ACCORDING TO YOUR ANIMAL SIGN

*T*here are certain days of the Chinese month that are more auspicious and some days less auspicious for individuals based on the animal sign under which they are born. For each animal sign there are three favourable days each month and three unfavourable days. The three favourable days will be excellent for you to pursue activities related to your career, your work (business) and your marriage or partnership. These are the days when your potential for success, power and upward mobility can take root or ripen. The three unfavourable days are days when you could well succumb to obstacles, aggravations and people with bad intentions towards you. These are the days when you are weak so these are days when you should lie low and not engage in verbal or physical contact with your enemies.

The Table here shows you how to find the auspicious and inauspicious days of the month for you based on your animal sign. The numbered days indicated in the table refer to the Chinese days of the month and here we are NOT referring to the HSIA month but to the lunar month. To obtain the Chinese lunar months you will need to refer to the new moon in the annual Almanac Calendar published by **wofs.com**. The new moon day always sounds as DAY 1 of the lunar month. All other days follow from this first day.

Always try to select one of your three favourable days to embark on projects whose success is important to you. It can be related to your work or to your heart – the vibrations of certain days being luckier for people according to their animal signs is related to most people it is during the time of the waxing or expanding moon that seems more favourable i.e. that their success days fall within the first fifteen days of the month. The exception to this seems to be the 27th day for gaining power for those born under animal signs Tiger, Rabbit, and Dog. For the Rooster also

AUSPICIOUS & INAUSPICIOUS DAYS BY ANIMAL SIGN OF YEAR OF BIRTH

	RAT	OX	TIGER	RABBIT	DRAGON	SNAKE
LUCKY	20th Day	17th Day	5th Day	11th Day	3rd Day	13th Day
POWER	6th Day	14th Day	27th Day	27th Day	12th Day	12th Day
SUCCESS	3rd Day	12th Day	9th Day	12th Day	17th Day	6th Day
OBSTACLE	26th Day	12th Day	14th Day	26th Day	8th Day	8th Day
AGGRAVATION	10th Day	18th Day	12th Day	25th Day	9th Day	9th Day
ENEMY	23rd Day	5th Day	3rd Day	18th Day	11th Day	6th Day

	HORSE	SHEEP	MONKEY	ROOSTER	DOG	BOAR
LUCKY	17th Day	8th Day	8th Day	14th Day	9th Day	2nd Day
POWER	12th Day	1st Day	1st Day	7th Day	27th Day	8th Day
SUCCESS	6th Day	2nd Day	2nd Day	25th Day	5th Day	11th Day
OBSTACLE	20th Day	20th Day	9th Day	3rd Day	11th Day	26th Day
AGGRAVATION	5th Day	5th Day	10th Day	11th Day	3rd Day	3rd Day
ENEMY	27th Day	27th Day	17th Day	24th Day	12th Day	12th Day

the success day is the 25th day which falls within the period of the waning moon.

The characteristics and attributes of each of the thirty or so days of the lunar month indicates the success or obstacles that one will encounter during that day. New jobs, new projects and renovation works on one's homes should ideally be started during SUCCESS days and then the attainment of goals will be assured. On enemy days one should avoid everything to do with discussions, meetings, court cases and so forth otherwise the battles you fight could well be lost.

For activities related to increasing your power you should choose your POWER days – this means when you are standing for elections, applying for a job, going for an interview or pitching for a promotion or a contract. When election day falls on your POWER day you will surely be assured of success. Note that when the weekly and this monthly cycle of good and bad days contradict each other for the same day given to any individual, then **the weekly cycle is regarded as exerting the stronger influence and this is because the weekly cycles are ruled by the powerful planets**. When the two influences confirm each other then both must definitely be taken into ac count when making a judgement about days.

INFLUENCE OF ANIMAL SIGN OF EACH DAY

In the annual Almanac calendar which wofs.com publishes each year, the ruling element and ruling animal sign of the day for the 365 days of the year are shown in each of the monthly calendars. These days have specific characteristics associated with them and it is useful to take account of their attributes since these offer clues to the energies of the day. Here is a brief description of the attributes of days ruled by the twelve animal signs:

DAY OF THE RAT is favourable for engagements, marriages, the birth of a son, for trade and important projects. This is a day when fleshy contact should be avoided and it is also a good day to be a vegetarian. Today divinations done will be accurate and it is a good day to start a journey. The conflict animal is the Horse.

DAY OF THE OX is a good day for embarking on difficult and heavy tasks such as road works, building a house and making the effort to resolve problems. It is not so favourable for spiritual practices.

DAY OF THE TIGER is favourable for prosperity rituals such as making a wealth vase, building a water feature, starting a 49 day wish list or making fire rituals to symbolically cleanse all the negativities of your life. It is not a good day for marriages generally or for celebrations. Certainly not a good day to give birth.

DAY OF THE RABBIT is favourable for funerals, for royal occasions and for buying a pet.

DAY OF THE DRAGON

is favourable for religious practices, consecrations and for making pujas to get rid of negative forces in your life. This is an excellent day to ask for favours especially from people in higher authority than you. It is a great day to be courageous and brave. Faint heart never won fair lady applies to this day.

DAY OF THE SNAKE is a great day for making offerings and giving gifts to friends and relatives. It is also a good day to lend or borrow money. If you journey South on this day you will receive good news.

DAY OF THE HORSE

is auspicious for festivals, celebrations and for improving your relationships. It's a good time to keep in touch with overseas friends. This is a day when it is most unfavourable for cutting hair and for getting married. Contact with blood should be avoided at all costs.

DAY OF THE SHEEP

is a day that is suitable for ceremonies and for upgrading the household. Any work connected with the earth such as planting, building and digging is favourable. But this is not a good day to have surgery or for entering hospital.

DAY OF THE MONKEY is favourable

for all kinds of pleasurable activities, sports, music and games of chance. It is also good for marriage dinners and other celebrations. It is not a good day to get honoured or for accepting bigger responsibilities.

DAY OF THE ROOSTER is an

excellent day to prepare and take medicines i.e. go to hospital, give aid to those in need i.e. do charity work and for undertaking important communication work. It is a day when large festivals and celebrations are best avoided.

DAY OF THE DOG

is a favourable day for undertaking prosperity rituals and other prayers. It is a very bad day to cut or wash hair.

DAY OF THE BOAR is favourable

for the transmission and passing over of one's power and for welcoming

ceremonies. It is a good day to open a new building or launch a new product. However all contact with the earth should be avoided so no planting, digging or building.

PERSONALISED INTERPRETATIONS

Note that it is possible to make personalized readings of the element and animal sign of the day by looking at how the DAY's element and animal sign interacts with the element and animal sign of one's year of birth. Thus:

THE ELEMENTS

To determine if a certain day is favourable for you examine the element relationship between your self-element at birth with that of the day. If the day's element produces your self-element then the day is good for you. if the element is the same as your year of birth element it means the day brings friends. if the element destroys your element it means the day is bad for you and if the element exhausts your year element then it will be a very exhausting day.

COMPATIBITLITY OF ANIMAL SIGNS

When your year animal sign is friends with or allies with the animal sign of the day then the day is favourable. When the animal sign of the day is in conflict with your animal sign then the day will be very trying. The day is then not good and important activities should be avoided . You should also not make important decisions.

When the animals are the same, then any judgement you make becomes a matter of being very careful so you would be well advised to be prudent. Remember that when the animal sign is the same it can indicate either a friend OR an enemy.

Part Seven

READING OF SAMPLE CHARTS

Reading Of Sample Charts

CHART ONE

FOUR PILLARS

HOUR	DAY	MONTH	YEAR
壬 Yang Water	丙 Yang Fire	戊 Yang Earth	戊 Yang Earth
戊 辰 Yang Earth Dragon	戊 辰 Yang Earth Dragon	丙 午 Yang Fire Horse	丙 午 Yang Fire Horse

16	26	36	46	56	66
丙 Yang Fire	乙 Yin Wood	甲 Yang Wood	癸 Yin Water	壬 Yang Water	辛 Yin Metal
辰 Yang Earth Dragon	卯 Yin Wood Rabbit	寅 Yang Wood Tiger	丑 Yin Earth Ox	子 Yang Water Rat	亥 Yin Water Boar

Element	Areas of Life
EARTH	Inteligence, Creativity
FIRE	Friends, Foe, Colleagues, Competition
WATER	Recognition, Power, Rank
WOOD	Resource, Support, Authority
METAL	Wealth, Financial Success

CHART ONE:

ROSEMARY
FEMALE, EARTH HORSE
Currently 27 Years Old

FIVE TYPES OF LUCK
Wealth indicated by Metal
Intelligence indicated by Earth
Resources indicated by Wood
Friends/competitors indicated by Fire
Recognition/power indicated by Water

BASKET OF ELEMENTS:
4 earth; 3 fire, 1 water
missing Wood & Metal
No direct and obvious indication of wealth
Shortage of resources luck. No hidden
stems or branches

SELF ELEMENT is **Yang fire. WEAK**
FAVOURABLE ELEMENTS -
wood & metal and water

UNFAVORABLE ELEMENT -
earth (too much earth in the chart)

PHASES OF LIFE LUCK
Her FATE luck is indicated by Yang FIRE
Her Coming of Age element is Wood

READING BASED ON ABOVE

1. Based on an analysis of the different phases of her life, she benefits from OPPORTUNITY LUCK during her Coming of Age phase, which begins around the time she is 26 years old (indicated from her Luck Pillars chart). From 26 all through to 46 years ie for a period of 20 years she benefits from her luck pillars of WOOD. So she has just entered her excellent period, which gets better after 36 years and lasts until 46. She should really make the most of this period of her life because she is just entering into her best period when everything succeeds. At both professional and personal level she will experience happiness and fulfillment. She is not short of support, money or friendships.

2. This is because we have seen that she is weak fire desperately short of resources ie WOOD. She needs WOOD to strengthen her self-element so she benefits very much during these twenty years when WOOD dominates

her luck pillars. We know that WOOD is both her RESOURSES as well as her OPPORTUNITY luck indicator. So the element brings a double positive benefit. This is a rare occurrence in the chart and is deemed to be a very auspicious indicator of good fortune.

3. Because her self element is Yang Fire, she will benefit more from her Yang wood pillar years i.e. from the age 36 to 46 years.

4. Because WOOD is her Opportunity luck she will benefit form the element doing creative work such as dancing or the performing arts. The more creative her work is the more she will flourish and benefit form her destiny. If she works in the performing arts she will have great success.

5. As for her marriage luck, she should get married after the age of 26 years. If she marries before this age she will have a great deal of mental anguish and sufferings. After she has passed 26 years she will be happier in her marriage. However note that her Earthly branch in the MONTH Pillar creates hidden Yin earth and this will affect her judgment and her mental state. It is not a good indication as it suggests some problems brought by the older generation i.e. from Dad or Mum or in-laws.

6. Her chart shows that she will bring indirect benefits to her spouse and her spouse will exhaust her.

7. Around the age of 46 she will experience a traumatic event that can cause her to change her life, her lifestyle or direction in life. The Change need not be negative as the element represented by her FATE luck which brings this about is FIRE which strengthens her. According to Paht Chee, when the FATE element is FIRE it suggests a change of direction in one's career, perhaps a transfer, a new job or being made an amazing offer which one finds hard to refuse. It will however be a job that brings friends and competitors alike into her life. This is a stage of her life when she will have to make some tough decisions.

8. From age 51 to 56 she will suffer mental anguish and stress. A great deal of unhappiness is indicated related to the husband and children. She has to cope with problems brought about by betrayal and worry of some kind. From age 56 onwards for another ten years she will turn her mind towards spiritual pursuits and this will offer some comfort. But her FAMILY luck period is indicated by the element of EARTH which is unfavorable for her and this suggests that her turning inwards towards herself is brought on by suffering.

9. Materially however she has no worry since there is both Water and Metal in her luck pillars during the later years of her life i.e. from 46 trough to 56 onwards. Since these are her favourable elements it suggest that she will be well off materially. More, these elements indicate WEALTH and RECOGNITION so she has money and the respect of her peers and community during her old age. In other words she retires very well off indeed.

10. To sum up therefore this is a good chart which shows success at the prime of her life. She may not be seriously wealthy then but as she grows older wealth and recognition comes to her. It is only during the five years between 51 to 56 years of age that she suffers a small period of unhappiness but after that it is good again. The entrée of spirituality into her life will also bring great happiness.

HOW TO ENHANCE HER DESTINY

1. She benefits from the Wood element which brings the vitally needed resource luck into her life so she should wear green coloured stones such as emeralds and jade. It would benefit her greatly to wear a jade mystical knot close to her body at all times.

2. Through her life and especially during the difficult years 51 to 56 years she will benefit from wearing lots of jewellery to emphasize the metal element. Metal exhausts the earth element that is bringing her grief. But wood is better so her home is best designed to incorporate lots of wood energy.

CHART TWO:

DARYL
MALE, EARTH MONKEY
Currently 37 years old.

FIVE TYPES OF LUCK
Wealth indicated by EARTH
Intelligence indicated by FIRE
Resources indicated by WATER
Friends/competitors indicated by WOOD
Recognition/power indicated by METAL

BASKET OF ELEMENTS:
3 metal; 2 earth; 2 wood; 1 water and
missing FIRE
EXCELLENT indication of recognition
& wealth luck. Shortage of resources
luck. No hidden stems or branches.

SELF ELEMENT is **Yin wood. WEAK**
Favourable elements – water and fire (lacking
of FIRE)
Unfavorable element – METAL and EARTH
(Metal hurts self element and earth
produces metal)

PHASES OF LIFE LUCK
His FATE luck is indicated by Yang METAL
(MONKEY)
His Coming of Age element is FIRE (Prosperity)
then OPPORTUNITY, then FATE.

SPECIAL STARS IN CHART:
1. Nobleman star – help comes from influential people. Rat & Monkey years are excellent.
2. Warrior Star – harms the wife. Misfortune to his spouse is indicated – can also indicate permanent separation. (Cure is to suppress metal of the HOUR pillar Monkey with water)

CONDENSED READING
1. He enters his good period at the age of 39 years when the much needed missing element of FIRE to provide warmth to this autumn wood person features strongly and lasts five years until 44 years of age. After that the pillar changes to yang wood, which suggests he could enter into a romantic affair that can become serious between 44 to 49 years of age.

2. In the year 2013 in a water snake year when he is 45 years old and entering his luck pillar of WOOD he will enjoy incredible success. This is a year when he is strong and his mental capabilities are at a peak. His wealth luck is sure to manifest. His chart reveals he has wealth luck (earth element). In that year also, the Snake combines very well with the Monkey, being secret friends.

CHART TWO

FOUR PILLARS

HOUR	DAY	MONTH	YEAR
甲 Yang Wood	乙 Yin Wood	壬 Yang Water	戊 Yang Earth
庚申 Yang Metal Monkey	辛酉 Yin Metal Rooster	戊戌 Yang Earth Dog	庚申 Yang Metal Monkey

19	29	39	49	59	69
甲 Yang Wood	乙 Yin Wood	丙 Yang Fire	丁 Yin Fire	戊 Yang Earth	己 Yin Earth
子 Yang Water Rat	丑 Yin Earth Ox	寅 Yang Wood Tiger	卯 Yin Wood Rabbit	辰 Yang Earth Dragon	巳 Yin Fire Snake

Element	Areas of Life
FIRE	Inteligence, Creativity
WOOD	Friends, Foe, Colleagues, Competition
METAL	Recognition, Power, Rank
WATER	Resource, Support, Authority
EARTH	Wealth, Financial Success

午未申酉戌亥
子丑寅卯辰巳

己庚辛壬癸
甲乙丙丁戊

This combination brings him excellent speculative luck. If he takes risk or gambles he will reap a big bonanza this year.

3. From 49 to 54 he benefits from fire but the yin fire brings excellent direct benefit to his self-element of Yin wood. His self-element was very weak at time of birth due to the coming of winter indicating a need for fire. Note also that the whole chart lacks fire. Hence fire becomes a crucial requirement for his success and well being. His surroundings should always be kept well lit.

4. At age 49 in the year 2017, the elements of this fire rooster year - metal and fire – brings serious recognition luck. In 2019 The yin water PIG makes an appearance in the calendar and this is when his luck really blossoms. This will be a very special year for him.

5. He has the star of the Nobleman in his chart and this is a positive indication since this suggests that he will always have get help from helpful people. This reinforces the good fortune that is brought to him by his YEAR animal sign of Monkey so every time the Monkey comes around he enjoys good fortune (as in 2004).

6. The warrior star in his chart hurts his spouse as its appearance is caused by the combination of the HOUR MONKEY with the DAY ROOSTER. This indicates a clash of egos between yin and yang metal in the two pillars that suggest husband and wife. It suggests there could be a permanent rift which occurs between the ages of 34 to the present. It is likeliest to occur in a Tiger year or when the stem of the year is metal.

7. In times of timing, his coming of age luck is PROSPERITY this means that from 19 years onwards he will experience increased income levels. So from the start of his working life he becomes financially successful. His prosperity is FIRE and this indicates that the source of his wealth comes from the corporate world or from his own entrepreneurial skills. FIRE always suggests business and things commercial, for the energy of fire is soaring and upward so he has excellent business luck. his success comes from there.

8. His OPPORTUNITY luck comes around the Maturity phase and for him, because the element is earth, it indicates that opportunity comes in the form of a new job requiring a relocation to another industry or even another country. But whatever it is he should take it as it indicates enormous success.

APPENDICES

THE TEN HEAVENLY STEMS

The ten heavenly stems are central to the eight characters chart and they occupy the top half of the Four Pillars in the chart. Basically they signify the five elements of wood, fire, earth, metal and water in a yin as well as a yang aspect. For students of *paht chee* or *eight characters*, once you have a good general idea of how the chart is to be read and analyzed, you can go deeper into the meanings, characteristics and attributes of heavenly stems. These stems are fundamental codes that contain a wealth of information for interpretation and deductions as to the fortunes of individuals. Although the interpretation relies almost exclusively on the productive and destructive relationships between the elements, the quality of one's readings depends on a full understanding of the attributes of the five elements, as well as the important role played by whether it manifests in a yin aspect or a yang aspect. The ten heavenly stems and their elements are described herewith:

1 JIA (甲) YANG WOOD

WOOD is the only element that is alive and has a life of its own. So **yang wood** stresses the living aspect of the wood energy. An excellent way to view this heavenly stem is to think of a large tree, which grows upwards strong and healthy. This growth aspect of the tree indicates the quality of hard work and industrious effort and can suggest someone highly motivated. However the solid trunk and straight upward growth direction also

FIVE ELEMENTS	YANG ELEMENTS	YIN ELEMENTS
WOOD	1. JIA	2. YI
FIRE	3. BING	4. DING
EARTH	5. WU	6. JI
METAL	7. GENG	8. XIN
WATER	9. REN	10. GUI

signifies someone rather inflexible and dogmatic and stubborn. So if the self-element is Yang wood, and if it is weak, it will manifest the more positive qualities and if it is strong it can manifest a stubborn streak, or it can suggest someone who is righteous and uncompromising to the point of being difficult.

Next note that the large canopy of leaves provides shade and this can be translated into the quality of benevolence and compassion as it provides shelter. The tree is usually slow growing so it suggests patience. Thus yang wood indicates a person who is kind and compassionate always ready to lend a helping hand. The roots of a large tree goes deep into the ground suggesting a strong foundation that results in stability. So this describes someone who is down to earth and stable, a person who works meticulously and has a strong character. These qualities reflect all the positive aspects of yang wood, but the negative side suggests that there is inflexibility and resistance to change.

How we interpret the presence of YANG WOOD in the chart depends on the elements of the other heavenly stems, and on their yin or yang manifestations."

2 YI (乙) YIN WOOD

Yin wood is wood of a lesser robust quality. Yin wood is smaller, less vigorous and less imposing. Its growth is even slower and its character is milder, gentler and a great deal more tactful reflecting its female aspect. Yin wood is yielding and soft while yang wood is strong and aggressive. Its upward growth is meandering and curving, finding ways round obstacles and yielding to them rather than fighting directly. A person with yin wood as the **self element** will usually have a gentle and milder disposition, using tact rather than strong words to get his/her way. Because of its yin nature which tends to be darker and lacking in light, a yin wood person will always seek out the yang, so in the form of wood energy, this person will keep on climbing upwards in search of sunlight. So it will give in to others in order to satisfy himself/herself.

Yin wood is also characterized by an attitude of flexibility, swaying according to the wind directions. They appear fragile but by going with the flow of the wind they are in reality rather hardy. Think of the blade of grass and the mighty oak tree in the face of a storm. The grass blade is unaffected while the oak can get uprooted.

This analogy is very telling as it emphasizes that in softness there can sometimes be more strength than in being hard and tough.

3 BING (丙) YANG FIRE

This is big and active fire energy and It is usually associated with bright sunlight which brings warmth and radiance to the Universe. The sun shines in all directions and it can be scorchingly hot when one gets too near. When the self element is yang Fire it suggests a person who radiates warmth and brightness. This is a person who is honest, passionate and upright when he/she starts life.

As the person grows into adulthood other influences come into play and the yang fire person can change. But the innate nature of such a person is that he/she is seldom petty, almost always generous, has boundless energy and is happiest when kept busy and working hard.

A yang fire person is generally cheerful and magnanimous to one and all, neither differentiating according to class or status nor being influenced by race or other differences. Because the **self-element** is fire this person usually shines forth and is easily the center of attraction.

On the negative side yang fire does suggest instability of emotions. Like the flames that soar and wane, likewise a yang fire person can also be rather unpredictable.

4 DING (丁) YIN FIRE

This suggest small fire, that created by a candle or by a torchlight or a camp fire. It is small but it still radiates warmth and embraces all who surround it with a warm glow. Because it is yin, its demeanour is gentle and rather more concentrated.

Those whose self element is Yin fire tend to be outwardly affectionate to those they love, and seem to be always willing to go out on a limb for them. Such people tend to be focused rather like a laser beam of light, penetrating and targeted.

When the self-element is weak yin fire, it suggests that the person is easily taken advantage of. This is because a yin fire person has no subterfuge and almost always wears the heart on the sleeve in full view of everyone. This person cannot successfully hide his/her true feelings.

As a result as this person matures into adulthood, they will tend to be wary and suspicious of people's motives.

5 WU (戊) YANG EARTH

At its most yang, this heavenly stem can signify the world, the planet earth, all the rocks and boulders, all the mountains and valleys of the world.

Earth is the one element that there is no shortage of as the whole world comprise earth chi energy. Yang earth hides many resources, and in fact it hides so many things that one can get quite overwhelmed.

If your **self element** is the heavenly stem Yang earth, it implies a very mysterious personality which has the potential to hide many things. It can also suggest someone with a very magnanimous nature.

The yang earth person indicates earth on the move − think of earthquakes, volcanic eruptions and the like and you get an idea of the kind of energy we are dealing with here. Earth in its natural state does not move. Earth stays silent and still most of the time but when it moves it creates massive repercussions. Think of a mountain moving!

So it is with people whose self element is yang earth. They do not speak much nor do they take action much but when they do they cause a rumble. Such people tend to be very powerful but offer few insights into the way they think or in what they believe in. It is hard to know which side they are on as they play their cards close to their chest.

Yang earth people are the most covert people in the Universe. But surprisingly they are also amongst the most trustworthy.

Those whose self element is weak yang earth will not be as true to type as those with strong yang earth.

6 JI (己) YIN EARTH

This is earth element manifested in more manageable proportions. So it resembles the soil, small boulders and stones, and of course, crystals in all their magnificence.

If your **self element** is Yin earth you are likely to be possessive, rather motherly and automatically taking on the matriarchal role in any situation.

Like the soil which transforms water and minerals into nurturing plant food for all the plants of the world, a yin wood person will likewise nurture those around them, especially their protégés, their children and their employees. So there is a very fierce manifestation of the mother instinct.

When the **self element** is weak, the indications are a dependence on traditional and conservative viewpoints. Such a person need others to be brave in trying out new things and adapting to change.

When the self element is strong, it manifests as the big mama taking charge of everyone and demonstrating a heart that is as big as the world.

7 GENG (庚) YANG METAL

The image here is of unbending energy. Yang metal connotes weapons of destruction such as tanks and guns and swords – tough, unbending and killing. When your self element is yang metal you will come across direct, resilient, stiff and determined to appear strong and tough.

Superficially the yang metal self element person is hard rather than tough, unbending rather than stubborn.

This is an element that has no life. It is merely a substance but a hard substance so they are unbending.

So they are often ruled by the belief systems and the principles which have been ingrained into them either since their childhood or systematically schooled into them. They will tend to reject change

and do not look kindly on compromise.

When the self element is weak the unbending nature of their character is less pronounced, making them less rigid. When the self element that is yang metal is strong, they will be difficult to deal with.

8 XIN (辛) YIN METAL

Yin metal is usually associated with precious gold, ie metal which has been worked on and changed into objects of value. ,

People whose **self-element** is Yin gold tend to be elegant and charming but they tend to place great importance on material possessions. As such they can exhibit a rather greedy and acquisitive disposition.

This is not necessarily always such a bad thing because those whose self element is strong will be motivated by their attachments to material possessions while those whose self element is weak will tend to succumb to temptations. They are more easily "bought" by those seeking their favour.

People whose self element is yin metal are seldom unbending but they are less able to cope when obstacles materialize in their life.

9 REN (壬) YANG WATER

This is big water and it generally refers to water which has a life of its own. Think of the vast waterfalls of the world – those that have roaring waters that flow and move along aggressively in a forward direction. At its zenith yang water can be rather destructive so when the **self element** of yang water is strong, it suggests an energy so strong it can literally sweep you into oblivion.

When water is strong it must be controlled and its energy must be exhausted. Otherwise it will not only destroy itself it also sweeps others along with it. The destructive power of water can be dangerous.

When the **self element** of yang water is weak however, it suggests that the water is under control and in this context the indications are favourable. Water brings with a great many things picked up along the way as it flows unrelentingly downward.

Yang water is water that has life such as living things like fish and other water creatures. It also indicates the presence of plants and other vegetation. Yang water is akin to the special universe of a flowing river which flows on irrespective of obstacles in its way or changes of season.

So yang water suggests a person who is very adaptable who can overcome almost any obstacle. It suggests a resilience and a determination that is most praiseworthy.

10 GUI (癸) YIN WATER

Yin water is water that has no life. So it suggests still water such as swamps and bodies of water that stay still, hiding many things beneath its surface. When your **self element** is yin water, it suggests someone mysterious and foreboding.

Such water however is not necessarily totally lifeless – it only appears so. Beneath its still exterior there can lie many unknown things. But appearance wise this person will show a calm disposition even though in reality he may be harbouring all kinds of thoughts.

Yin water can also be likened to dew drops – tiny drops of still water that appear fragile but which can infuse into many things. If your self-element is weak and it is Yin water, it can suggest that you worry too much and your attitude towards life is excessively pessimistic.

If your **self-element** is strong, it suggests that your calm exterior is supported by a belief in yourself. You are a more optimistic person.

THE TWELVE EARTHLY BRANCHES

*T*he lower section of the eight characters chart comprise the combinations of the twelve earthly branches which are more easily recognized when described as the twelve animals signs of the Chinese Zodiac. These branches should actually be seen as the roots of the heavenly stems, roots that are buried deep in the earth. Like the stems the branches also have yin and yang aspects, and they possess intrinsic elements too. The table below summarizes the earthly branches of the eight characters chart.

NAME	ZODIAC	MONTH*	ELEMENT	YIN/YANG	BODY PART
ZI	RAT	1ST	WATER	YANG	BLADDER
CHOU	OX	2ND	EARTH	YIN	SPLEEN
YIN	TIGER	3RD	WOOD	YANG	BILE DUCT
MAO	RABBIT	4TH	WOOD	YIN	LIVER
CHEN	DRAGON	5TH	EARTH	YANG	BELLY
SI	SNAKE	6TH	FIRE	YIN	HEART
WU	HORSE	7TH	FIRE	YANG	INTESTINE(S)
WEI	SHEEP	8TH	EARTH	YIN	SPLEEN
SHEN	MONKEY	9TH	METAL	YANG	INTESTINE(B)
YOU	ROOSTER	10TH	METAL	YIN	LUNGS
XU	DOG	11TH	EARTH	YANG	STOMACH
HAI	BOAR	12TH	WATER	YIN	KIDNEY

* in eight characters the months refer to the lunar months.

COMBINATION & CLASHES

1 HEAVENLY STEMS PRODUCED BY COMBINATION OF EARTHLY BRANCHES

According to the texts on eight characters, the energy of the earthly branches are far more complicated than those of the heavenly stems. The earthly branches have principal chi energies as well as residual chi energies and these also exert their influences on the *eight characters* chart. The residual energies can be detected by looking at the MONTH pillar of the eight characters chart. Here one can one can look for **heavenly stems** hidden inside the MONTH earthly branch.

MONTH EARTHLY BRANCH	MAIN CHI ENERGY	HEAVENLY STEM (HIDDEN)	HEAVENLY STEM (HIDDEN)
TIGER	Yang Wood	Yang Earth	Yang Fire
RABBIT	Yin Wood	Nil	Nil
DRAGON	Yang Earth	Yin Water	Yin Wood
SNAKE	Yin Fire	Yang Earth	Yang Metal
HORSE	Yang Fire	Yin Earth	Nil
SHEEP	Yin Earth	Yin Wood	Yin Fire
MONKEY	Yang Metal	Yang Earth	Yang Metal
ROOSTER	Yin Metal	Nil	Nil
DOG	Yang Earth	Yin Fire	Yin Metal
BOAR	Yin Water	Yang Wood	Nil
RAT	Yang Water	Nil	Nil
OX	Yin Earth	Yin Metal	Yin Water

The hidden heavenly stem offers an additional element for analysis of the chart. If they are favourable to the self element (the heavenly stem of the DAY pillar) they strengthen the chart and if they are unfavorable they can trigger unpleasant events to manifest OR they can cause auspicious stars to turn malevolent.

2 CLASH OF THE EARTHLY BRANCHES & HEAVENLY STEMS

These occur under two circumstances:

a) When the elements of the stems placed next to each other are **destructive** in nature eg. as in wood and metal; metal and fire, fire and water; water and earth; and earth and wood. It is deemed a conflict only when the elements belong to the same yin or yang essence. Hence heavenly stem JIA (yang wood) conflicts with GENG (yang metal) but is not in conflict with XIN (yin metal).

b) When the elements of the branches placed next to each other are destructive or opposite in nature eg. as in MAO (rabbit yin wood) and YOU (rooster yin metal). Another example is SHEN (Horse yang fire) and YIN (rat yang water).

These clashes are direct and obvious and they will cause obstacles to manifest when they appear in the luck pillars and cause the auspicious special stars to turn unfavourable.

However a clash can also have the effect of nullifying the effect of an unfavorable element. This happens when the element that is "destroyed" is unfavorable to the self element. By the same token if the element that gets 'destroyed" is a favourable element, then the effect is inauspicious.

3 SIX AUSPICIOUS COMBINATIONS OF THE EARTHLY BRANCHES

These are the six combinations of the secret friends of the Zodiac. When these occur together in the eight characters chart, or in the ten year luck periods next to each other it is an auspicious indication. It is also important to take note of the resultant element created and if this is also favourable to the self-element then the auspicious nature of the combination is magnified.

This translates into excellent good fortune. In the eight characters chart what it signifies depends on what the element means for you. Thus if the element created means wealth luck then it suggests wealth luck is considerably strengthened, if it denotes resources luck then it means that your resources gets expanded. For purposes of interpretation always go back to basics, to the all important self element, the favourable and unfavorable elements and to what each of the elements mean in your chart. The six auspicious combinations and the element created is illustrated above:

SIX AUSPICIOUS COMBINATIONS OF EARTHLY BRANCHES

COMBINATION OF	ELEMENT CREATED
Horse & Sheep	Fire
Snake & Monkey	Water
Dragon & Rooster	Metal
Rabbit & Dog	Fire
Tiger & Boar	Wood
Rat & Ox	Earth

FOUR AUSPICIOUS COMBINATIONS OF EARTHLY BRANCHES

ALLIES COMBINATION	ELEMENT CREATED
Snake & Rooster & Ox	Metal
Dragon & Monkey & Rat	Water
Sheep & Boar & Rabbit	Wood
Tiger & Horse & Dog	Fire

4 FOUR AUSPICIOUS COMBINATIONS OF EARTHLY BRANCHES

These are the four combinations of the zodiac allies, which when they occur close together in the eight characters chart, or in the ten year luck periods next to each other is also regarded as an auspicious indication.

It is also important to take note of the resultant element created and if this is also favourable to the self-element then the auspicious nature of the combination is magnified. When the resultant element created is unfavorable it does not nullify the good luck but it reduces it.

In the eight characters chart what it signifies depends on what the element means for you. Thus if the element created means wealth luck then it suggests wealth luck is considerably strengthened, if it denotes resources luck then it means that your resources gets expanded. For purposes of interpretation always go back to basics, to the all-important self element, the favourable and unfavorable elements and to what each of the elements mean in your chart.

5 SEASONAL COMBINATION OF THE EARTHLY BRANCHES

The seasonal combination of the earthly branches is deemed to be one of the most powerful indications in the *eight characters* chart and its appearance is considered strong enough to overcome all other indications.

Thus the seasonal combinations of the earthly branches are described as being

SEASONAL COMBINATION OF EARTHLY BRANCHES

SEASONAL COMBINATION OF	ELEMENT CREATED	SEASON	DIRECTION
Tiger & Rabbit & Dragon	Wood	Spring	East
Snake & Horse & Sheep	Fire	Summer	South
Monkey & Rooster & Dog	Metal	Autumn	West
Boar & Rat & Ox	Water	Winter	North

a principal factor in determining the destiny direction of the chart. A seasonal combination is said to appear when all three of the required earthly branches appear in any of the four pillars and in whatever sequence.

The occurrence of the seasonal combination in the *eight characters* chart indicate that in terms of one's professional career it brings the help of someone very powerful; in one's business it brings financial aid and assistance either in the form of cooperation from unexpected quarters or it brings some excellent partners.

For relationships it brings the promise of excellent friends and for those who are single this combination brings a like minded potential spouse. So it spells marriage, good friendships and important meetings.

If the resultant element created is unfavorable the effect can be inauspicious. However the impact is not as great in its negative aspect as in its positive aspect.

6 SIX UNLUCKY COMBINATIONS OF EARTHLY BRANCHES

Finally, it is useful to take note of the natural "enemies" amongst the 12 earthly branch animals. When these occur close to each other it suggests a "clash" which results in the introduction of a negative consequence the reading in the *eight characters* chart. The effect is harmful when the two branches are next to each other as when it occurs in the YEAR and MONTH pillar's or in the MONTH and DAY pillars or when it occurs in the DAY and HOUR pillars. When they are not next to each other the effect is insignificant. The combinations of enemy are as follows:

DRAGON with DOG
ROOSTER with RABBIT
HORSE with RAT
SHEEP with OX
MONKEY with TIGER
PIG with SNAKE

ANIMAL	CHINESE NEW YEAR DATES		EARTHLY BRANCH	HEAVENLY STEM
Rat (Water)	FEB 5, 1924	- JAN 23, 1925	WATER	WOOD
Ox (Earth)	JAN 24, 1925	- FEB 12, 1926	EARTH	WOOD
Tiger (Wood)	FEB 13, 1926	- FEB 1, 1927	WOOD	FIRE
Rabbit (Wood)	FEB 2, 1927	- JAN 22, 1928	WOOD	FIRE
Dragon (Earth)	JAN 23, 1928	- FEB 9, 1929	EARTH	EARTH
Snake (Fire)	FEB 10, 1929	- JAN 29, 1930	FIRE	EARTH
Horse (Fire)	JAN 30, 1930	- FEB 16, 1931	FIRE	METAL
Sheep (Earth)	FEB 17, 1931	- FEB 5, 1932	EARTH	METAL
Monkey (Metal)	FEB 6, 1932	- JAN 25, 1933	METAL	WATER
Rooster (Metal)	JAN 26, 1933	- FEB 13, 1934	METAL	WATER
Dog (Earth)	FEB 14, 1934	- FEB 3, 1935	EARTH	WOOD
Boar (Water)	FEB 4, 1935	- JAN 23, 1936	WATER	WOOD
Rat (Water)	JAN 24, 1936	- FEB 10, 1937	WATER	FIRE
Ox (Earth)	FEB 11, 1937	- JAN 30, 1938	EARTH	FIRE
Tiger (Wood)	JAN 31, 1938	- FEB 18, 1939	WOOD	EARTH
Rabbit (Wood)	FEB 19, 1939	- FEB 7, 1940	WOOD	EARTH
Dragon (Earth)	FEB 8, 1940	- JAN 26, 1941	EARTH	METAL
Snake (Fire)	JAN 27, 1941	- FEB 14, 1942	FIRE	METAL
Horse (Fire)	FEB 15, 1942	- FEB 4, 1943	FIRE	WATER
Sheep (Earth)	FEB 5, 1943	- JAN 24, 1944	EARTH	WATER
Monkey (Metal)	JAN 25, 1944	- FEB 12, 1945	METAL	WOOD
Rooster (Metal)	FEB 13, 1945	- FEB 1, 1946	METAL	WOOD
Dog (Earth)	FEB 2, 1946	- JAN 21, 1947	EARTH	FIRE
Boar (Water)	JAN 22, 1947	- FEB 9, 1948	WATER	FIRE
Rat (Water)	FEB 10, 1948	- JAN 28, 1949	WATER	EARTH

ANIMAL	CHINESE NEW YEAR DATES	EARTHLY BRANCH	HEAVENLY STEM
Ox (Earth)	JAN 29, 1949 - FEB 16, 1950	EARTH	EARTH
Tiger (Wood)	FEB 17, 1950 - FEB 5, 1951	WOOD	METAL
Rabbit (Wood)	FEB 6, 1951 - JAN 26, 1952	WOOD	METAL
Dragon (Earth)	JAN 27, 1952 - FEB 13, 1953	EARTH	WATER
Snake (Fire)	FEB 14, 1953 - FEB 2, 1954	FIRE	WATER
Horse (Fire)	FEB 3, 1954 - JAN 23, 1955	FIRE	WOOD
Sheep (Earth)	JAN 24, 1955 - FEB 11, 1956	EARTH	WOOD
Monkey (Metal)	FEB 12, 1956 - JAN 30, 1957	METAL	FIRE
Rooster (Metal)	JAN 31, 1957 - FEB 17, 1958	METAL	FIRE
Dog (Earth)	FEB 18, 1958 - FEB 7, 1959	EARTH	EARTH
Boar (Water)	FEB 8, 1959 - JAN 27, 1960	WATER	EARTH
Rat (Water)	JAN 28, 1960 - FEB 14, 1961	WATER	METAL
Ox (Earth)	FEB 15, 1961 - FEB 4, 1962	EARTH	METAL
Tiger (Wood)	FEB 5, 1962 - JAN 24, 1963	WOOD	WATER
Rabbit (Wood)	JAN 25, 1963 - FEB 12, 1964	WOOD	WATER
Dragon (Earth)	FEB 13, 1964 - FEB 1, 1965	EARTH	WOOD
Snake (Fire)	FEB 2, 1965 - JAN 20, 1966	FIRE	WOOD
Horse (Fire)	JAN 21, 1966 - FEB 8, 1967	FIRE	FIRE
Sheep (Earth)	FEB 9, 1967 - JAN 29, 1968	EARTH	FIRE
Monkey (Metal)	JAN 30, 1968 - FEB 16, 1969	METAL	EARTH
Rooster (Metal)	FEB 17, 1969 - FEB 5, 1970	METAL	EARTH
Dog (Earth)	FEB 6, 1970 - JAN 26, 1971	EARTH	METAL
Boar (Water)	JAN 27, 1971 - FEB 14, 1972	WATER	METAL
Rat (Water)	FEB 15, 1972 - FEB 2, 1973	WATER	WATER
Ox (Earth)	FEB 3, 1973 - JAN 22, 1974	EARTH	WATER

ANIMAL	CHINESE NEW YEAR DATES	EARTHLY BRANCH	HEAVENLY STEM
Tiger (Wood)	JAN 23, 1974 - FEB 10, 1975	WOOD	WOOD
Rabbit (Wood)	FEB 11, 1975 - JAN 30, 1976	WOOD	WOOD
Dragon (Earth)	JAN 31, 1976 - FEB 17, 1977	EARTH	FIRE
Snake (Fire)	FEB 18, 1977 - FEB 6, 1978	FIRE	FIRE
Horse (Fire)	FEB 7, 1978 - JAN 27, 1979	FIRE	EARTH
Sheep (Earth)	JAN 28, 1979 - FEB 15, 1980	EARTH	EARTH
Monkey (Metal)	FEB 16, 1980 - FEB 4, 1981	METAL	METAL
Rooster (Metal)	FEB 5, 1981 - JAN 24, 1982	METAL	METAL
Dog (Earth)	JAN 25, 1982 - FEB 12, 1983	EARTH	WATER
Boar (Water)	FEB 13 1983 - FEB 1, 1984	WATER	WATER
Rat (Water)	FEB 2, 1984 - FEB 19, 1985	WATER	WOOD
Ox (Earth)	FEB 20, 1985 - FEB 8, 1986	EARTH	WOOD
Tiger (Wood)	FEB 9, 1986 - JAN 28, 1987	WOOD	FIRE
Rabbit (Wood)	JAN 29, 1987 - FEB 16, 1988	WOOD	FIRE
Dragon (Earth)	FEB 17, 1988 - FEB 5, 1989	EARTH	EARTH
Snake (Fire)	FEB 6, 1989 - JAN 26, 1990	FIRE	EARTH
Horse (Fire)	JAN 27, 1990 - FEB 14, 1991	FIRE	METAL
Sheep (Earth)	FEB 15, 1991 - FEB 3, 1992	EARTH	METAL
Monkey (Metal)	FEB 4, 1992 - JAN 22, 1993	METAL	WATER
Rooster (Metal)	JAN 23, 1993 - FEB 9, 1994	METAL	WATER
Dog (Earth)	FEB 10, 1994 - JAN 30, 1995	EARTH	WOOD
Boar (Water)	JAN 31, 1995 - FEB 18, 1996	WATER	WOOD
Rat (Water)	FEB 19, 1996 - FEB 6, 1997	WATER	FIRE
Ox (Earth)	FEB 7, 1997 - JAN 27, 1998	EARTH	FIRE
Tiger (Wood)	JAN 28, 1998 - FEB 15, 1999	WOOD	EARTH

ANIMAL	CHINESE NEW YEAR DATES	EARTHLY BRANCH	HEAVENLY STEM
Rabbit (Wood)	FEB 16, 1999 - FEB 4, 2000	WOOD	EARTH
Dragon (Earth)	FEB 5, 2000 - JAN 23, 2001	EARTH	METAL
Snake (Fire)	JAN 24, 2001 - FEB 11, 2002	FIRE	METAL
Horse (Fire)	FEB 12, 2002 - JAN 31, 2003	FIRE	WATER
Sheep (Earth)	FEB 1, 2003 - JAN 21, 2004	EARTH	WATER
Monkey (Metal)	JAN 22, 2004 - FEB 8, 2005	METAL	WOOD
Rooster (Metal)	FEB 9, 2005 - JAN 28, 2006	METAL	WOOD
Dog (Earth)	JAN 29, 2006 - FEB 17, 2007	EARTH	FIRE
Boar (Water)	FEB 18, 2007 - FEB 6, 2008	WATER	FIRE
Rat (Water)	**FEB 7, 2008 - JAN 25, 2009**	**WATER**	**EARTH**
Ox (Earth)	JAN 26, 2009 - FEB 13, 2010	EARTH	EARTH
Tiger (Wood)	FEB 14, 2010 - FEB 2, 2011	WOOD	METAL
Rabbit (Wood)	FEB 3, 2011 - JAN 22, 2012	WOOD	METAL
Dragon (Earth)	JAN 23, 2012 - FEB 9, 2013	EARTH	WATER
Snake (Fire)	FEB 10, 2013 - JAN 30, 2014	FIRE	WATER
Horse (Fire)	JAN 31, 2014 - FEB 18, 2015	FIRE	WOOD
Sheep (Earth)	FEB 19, 2015 - FEB 7, 2016	EARTH	WOOD
Monkey (Metal)	FEB 8, 2016 - JAN 27, 2017	METAL	FIRE
Rooster (Metal)	JAN 28, 2017 - FEB 15, 2018	METAL	FIRE
Dog (Earth)	FEB 16, 2018 - FEB 4, 2019	EARTH	EARTH
Boar (Water)	FEB 5, 2019 - JAN 24, 2020	WATER	EARTH
Rat (Water)	**JAN 25, 2020 - FEB 11, 2021**	**WATER**	**METAL**
Ox (Earth)	FEB 12, 2021 - JAN 31, 2022	EARTH	METAL
Tiger (Wood)	FEB 1, 2022 - JAN 21, 2023	WOOD	WATER
Rabbit (Wood)	JAN 22, 2023 - FEB 9, 2024	WOOD	WATER

ANIMAL	CHINESE NEW YEAR DATES		EARTHLY BRANCH	HEAVENLY STEM
Dragon (Earth)	FEB 10, 2024	- JAN 28, 2025	EARTH	WOOD
Snake (Fire)	JAN 29, 2025	- FEB 16, 2026	FIRE	WOOD
Horse (Fire)	FEB 17, 2026	- FEB 5, 2027	FIRE	FIRE
Sheep (Earth)	FEB 6, 2027	- JAN 25, 2028	EARTH	FIRE
Monkey (Metal)	JAN 26, 2028	- FEB 12, 2029	METAL	EARTH
Rooster (Metal)	FEB 13, 2029	- FEB 2, 2030	METAL	EARTH
Dog (Earth)	FEB 3, 2030	- JAN 22, 2031	EARTH	METAL
Boar (Water)	JAN 23, 2031	- FEB 10, 2032	WATER	METAL
Rat (Water)	FEB 11, 2032	- JAN 30, 2033	WATER	WATER
Ox (Earth)	JAN 31, 2033	- FEB 18, 2034	EARTH	WATER
Tiger (Wood)	FEB 19, 2034	- FEB 7, 2035	WOOD	WOOD
Rabbit (Wood)	FEB 8, 2035	- JAN 27, 2036	WOOD	WOOD
Dragon (Earth)	JAN 28, 2036	- FEB 14, 2037	EARTH	FIRE
Snake (Fire)	FEB 15, 2037	- FEB 3, 2038	FIRE	FIRE
Horse (Fire)	FEB 4, 2038	- JAN 23, 2039	FIRE	EARTH
Sheep (Earth)	JAN 24, 2039	- FEB 11, 2040	EARTH	EARTH
Monkey (Metal)	FEB 12, 2040	- JAN 31, 2041	METAL	METAL
Rooster (Metal)	FEB 1, 2041	- JAN 21, 2042	METAL	METAL
Dog (Earth)	JAN 22, 2042	- FEB 9, 2043	EARTH	WATER
Boar (Water)	FEB 10, 2043	- JAN 29, 2044	WATER	WATER
Rat (Water)	JAN 30, 2044	- FEB 16, 2045	WATER	WOOD
Ox (Earth)	FEB 17, 2045	- FEB 5, 2046	EARTH	WOOD
Tiger (Wood)	FEB 6, 2046	- JAN 25, 2047	WOOD	FIRE
Rabbit (Wood)	JAN 26, 2047	- FEB 13, 2048	WOOD	FIRE
Dragon (Earth)	FEB 14, 2048	- FEB 1, 2049	EARTH	EARTH

ANIMAL	CHINESE NEW YEAR DATES	EARTHLY BRANCH	HEAVENLY STEM
Snake (Fire)	FEB 2, 2049 - JAN 22, 2050	FIRE	EARTH
Horse (Fire)	JAN 23, 2050 - FEB 11, 2051	FIRE	METAL
Sheep (Earth)	FEB 12, 2051 - JAN 31, 2052	EARTH	METAL
Monkey (Metal)	FEB 1, 2052 - FEB 18, 2053	METAL	WATER
Rooster (Metal)	FEB 19, 2053 - FEB 7, 2054	METAL	WATER
Dog (Earth)	FEB 8, 2054 - JAN 27, 2055	EARTH	WOOD
Boar (Water)	JAN 28, 2055 - FEB 14, 2056	WATER	WOOD
Rat (Water)	FEB 15, 2056 - FEB 3, 2057	WATER	FIRE
Ox (Earth)	FEB 4, 2057 - JAN 23, 2058	EARTH	FIRE
Tiger (Wood)	JAN 24, 2058 - FEB 11, 2059	WOOD	EARTH
Rabbit (Wood)	FEB 12, 2059 - FEB 1, 2060	WOOD	EARTH
Dragon (Earth)	FEB 2, 2060 - JAN 20, 2061	EARTH	METAL
Snake (Fire)	JAN 21, 2061 - FEB 8, 2062	FIRE	METAL
Horse (Fire)	FEB 9, 2062 - JAN 28, 2063	FIRE	WATER
Sheep (Earth)	JAN 29, 2063 - FEB 16, 2064	EARTH	WATER
Monkey (Metal)	FEB 17, 2064 - FEB 4, 2065	METAL	WOOD
Rooster (Metal)	FEB 5, 2065 - JAN 25, 2066	METAL	WOOD
Dog (Earth)	JAN 26, 2066 - FEB 13, 2067	EARTH	FIRE
Boar (Water)	FEB 14, 2067 - FEB 2, 2068	WATER	FIRE

• *Where feng shui makes a difference* •

MALAYSIA

WOFS MID VALLEY
3rd Floor, Centre Court, K.L.
Tel: +603-2287 9975
Email: wofs@worldoffengshui.com

WOFS KL PLAZA
1st Floor, KL Plaza, K.L. Tel: +603-2148 2128
Email: wofs@worldoffengshui.com

WOFS MILENIUM
15th Floor, Menara Milenium, K.L.
Tel: +603-2080 3488
Email: wofs@worldoffengshui.com

WOFS 1 UTAMA
1st Floor, New Wing, P.J.
Tel: +603-7724 2248
Email: oneutama@worldoffengshui.com

WOFS KEPONG
Ground Floor, Jusco Metro
Prima Shopping Centre, Kepong, K.L.
Tel: +603-6250 0728
Email: kepong@worldoffengshui.com

WOFS CENTRAL MARKET
M34, Mezzanine Floor, Central Market, K.L.
Tel: +603-2274 8096
Email: wofs@worldoffengshui.com

WOFS ALOR SETAR
2nd Floor, Complex Star Parade, Kedah.
Tel: +604-730 8118
Email: alorsetar@worldoffengshui.com

WOFS BUKIT RAJA
Jusco Bukit Raja, Klang. Tel: +603-3341 3889
Email: bukitraja@worldoffengshui.com

WOFS GURNEY
Plaza Gurney, Penang, Malaysia.
Tel: +604-228 4618
Email: gurney@worldoffengshui.com

WOFS IPOH
Jalan Theatre, Ipoh, Perak.
Tel: +605-249 2688
Email: ipoh@worldoffengshui.com

WOFS JOHOR
Ground Floor, Jusco Permas Jaya Shopping
Centre, Johore Bahru. Tel: +607-388 9968
Email: johor@worldoffengshui.com

WOFS KOTA KINABALU
2nd Floor, Wisma Merdeka,
Kota Kinabalu, Sabah.
Tel: +088-248 798
Email: kotakinabalu@worldoffengshui.com

WOFS KUANTAN
1st Floor, Berjaya Megamall, Kuantan, Pahang.
Tel: +609-508 3168
Email: kuantan@worldoffengshui.com

WOFS KUCHING
Ground Floor, Wisma Ho Ho Lim,Kuching,
Sarawak, East Malaysia.
Tel: +082-425 698
Email: kuching@worldoffengshui.com

WOFS MELAKA
Mahkota Parade, Melaka.
Tel: +606-282 2688
Email: melaka@worldoffengshui.com

WOFS MUTIARA
Ground Floor, Mutiara Hotel Johor Bahru,
J.B. Johor. Tel: +607-331 9968
Email: johor@worldoffengshui.com

WOFS PUCHONG
2nd Floor, IOI Mall, Puchong, Selangor.
Tel: +603-5882 2652
Email: puchong@worldoffengshui.com

WOFS SEREMBAN
1st Floor, Jusco Shopping Centre Seremban 2,
Seremban. Tel: +606-601 3088
Email: seremban@worldoffengshui.com

WOFS SUBANG
Ground Floor, Subang Parade, P.J. Selangor.
Tel: +603-5632 1428
Email: subang@worldoffengshui.com

WOFS TAIPING
Taiping Business Centre, Taiping, Perak.
Tel: +605-806 6648
Email: taiping@worldoffengshui.com

WOFS TEBRAU
2nd Floor, Aeon Tebrau Shopping City
Shopping Centre No 1, J.B. Johor.
Tel: +607-357 9968
Email: johor@worldoffengshui.com

INTERNATIONAL

WOFS ARCADIA
Westfield Shopping Mall-Santa Anita,
Arcadia, CA, USA. Tel: +626 447 8886
Email: arcadia@worldoffengshui.com

WOFS ARTHA GADING
Artha Gading Mall, Gramedia Book Store
Jakarta-Utara. Tel: +6221-668 3610/20/30
Email: indonesia@worldoffengshui.com

WOFS BARCELONA
C.Urgell, Barcelona, Spain.
Tel: +34934244801
Email: spain@worldoffengshui.com

WOFS BELGIUM
Ninoofsesteenweg, Brussels, Belgium.
Tel: +32 02 522 2697
Email: belgium@worldoffengshui.com

WOFS BRUNEI
Warisan Mata-Mata, Brunei Darussalam.
Tel: +673-245 4977
Email: brunei@worldoffengshui.com

WOFS CALCUTTA
Shakespeare Sarani, Calcutta, India.
Tel: +9133-22815263
Email: calcutta@worldoffengshui.com

WOFS CEBU
Lower Ground Floor, SM City Cebu,
Philippines. Tel: +032 231 4088
Email: philippines@worldoffengshui.com

WOFS HAWAII
Kilohana Square, Honolulu, USA.
Tel: +1808-739-8288
Email: hawaii@worldoffengshui.com

WOFS JAPAN
S1 Nihonbashi Building SF 1-3-16 Nihonbashi
Horidomecho Chuocity Tokyo Japan.
Tel: +81-3-5645-6680
Email: japan@worldoffengshui.com

WOFS MIE
670-2 Shinmei Ago-Cho Shima-City, Mie,
517-0502, Japan. Tel: +81-599-43-8909
Email: mie@worldoffengshui.com

WOFS KELAPA GADING
Kelapa Gading Plaza,
Jakarta Indonesia. Tel: +6221-4526986
Email: indonesia@worldoffengshui.com

WOFS LAS VEGAS
Spring Mountain Blvd, Las Vegas, NV, USA.
Tel: +702-386-1888
Email: lasvegas@worldoffengshui.com

WOFS LONDON
Whiteleys Shopping Centre, Queensway.
Email: london@worldoffengshui.com

WOFS MADRID
Centro Comercial Mercado Puerta de Toledo,
Madrid, Spain. Tel: +34-91-3642771
Email: madrid@worldoffengshui.com

WOFS MATRAMAN
Toko Buku Gramedia Matraman,
Jakarta Timur, Indonesia.
Tel: +6221-8517325
Email: indonesia@worldoffengshui.com

WOFS MTA
Mall Taman Anggrek (MTA) Ground Level Lt.
Slipi-Jakarta Barat, Indonesia.
Tel: +6221-5699-9488
Email: indonesia@worldoffengshui.com

WOFS MELBOURNE
Lower Ground Floor, Crown Entertainment
Complex, Melbourne, Victoria, Australia.
Tel: +613-9645-8588
Email: melbourne@worldoffengshui.com

WOFS NETHERLANDS
Stationsplein 1, Netherlands.
Tel: +31-356781838
Email: netherlands@worldoffengshui.com

WOFS PHILIPPINES
Ground Floor, The Podium, Mandaluyong City,
Metro Manila, Philippines.
Tel: +63-29106000
Email: philippines@worldoffengshui.com

WOFS PLUIT
TB Gramedia Mega Mall Pluit, Jakarta Utara.
Tel: +6221-4586 4070
E-Mail: indonesia@worldoffengshui.com

WOFS THAILAND
10th Floor, Regent House, Bangkok, Thailand.
Tel: +66 (0) 2-254-9918, +66 (0) 2-254-7243,
+66 (0) 2-254-9540
Email: bangkok@worldoffengshui.com

WOFS SEACON SQUARE
2nd Floor, Seacon Square Department Store,
Thailand. Tel: +66 (0) 2-721-9398
Email: bangkok@worldoffengshui.com

WOFS TORONTO
Rutherford Road, Tuscany Place at Vaughan
Mills, Vaughan, Ontario, Canada.
Tel: +1 905 660 8899
Email: toronto@worldoffengshui.com

WOFS UNION MALL
F1 Union Mall Department Store 54,
Bangkok, Thailand.
Tel: +66(0)2-939-3268
Email: bangkok@worldoffengshui.com

WOFS VIETNAM
Cong Hoa, Ward 4 District Tan Binh, Ho Chi
Minh, Vietnam.
Email: vietnam@worldoffengshui.com

WOFS MOA
Mall of Asia, SM Central Business Park 1, Island
A, Bay City, Pasag City
Tel: +63-2910 6000
Email: philippines@worldoffengshui.com